# CLASS

# LESSONS

## *of*

# 1888

D1402464

# EMMA CURTIS HOPKINS

High
Watch

# CLASS

# LESSONS

# *of*

# 1888

WISEWOMAN
PRESS

Class Lessons of 1888 by Emma Curtis Hopkins

ISBN: 0-945385-07-2

Published 2006 by WiseWoman Press,
                    Portland, Oregon, USA


First  Printing, 2006.



Metaphysics
Religion
Spirituality/Health

Hopkins, Emma C. 1849-1925.

# Contents

# Foreword

The great American mystic, Emma Curtis Hopkins (1849-1925), brought forth a revelation of Truth that is still ahead of its time today. Her writings reflect the spiritual mountaintop of consciousness from which she lived and taught. Emma revealed a mysticism that was infused with practical application which provides for us an eternal, yet relevant, interpretation of the teachings of Jesus Christ.

This book, written towards the end of the nineteenth century, is a compilation of a lecture course she presented to her students at the Chicago Metaphysical Institute which she founded. As with her other writings, this book leads the reader from darkness to light, fear to faith, bondage to freedom and from sense consciousness to Christ Consciousness. She takes us on this journey with great clarity, deliberation and love. In so doing, she gives us the 'eyes to see and the ears to hear' what the Wisdom of the Ages has prepared for us.

I have been teaching from Emma's work for more than fifteen years. Her exalted consciousness has informed my entire ministry as well as the hearts and minds of the thousands of students I've had the privilege of serving. No single book, with the exception of the Holy Bible, has brought forth such continued illumination to my experience of life as the writings of Emma Curtis Hopkins.

I'm eternally grateful to beloved Emma for her writings and teachings. I'm also most grateful to the people who were instrumental in insuring that her teachings would be available to future students of Truth. Specifically, I'm grateful to DeVorss Publishing Company in Southern California for continuing to publish her two classics, *Scientific Christian Mental Practice* and *High Mysticism*. In addition, the late Rev. Marge Flotron of Chicago was an important leader in gathering Emma's lectures and writings into one place. Also, Rev. Shirley Lawrence, from Southern California, was instrumental in publishing Emma's three volume *Bible Interpretations* as well as what I believe to be her highest work and most comprehensive statement of her understanding, The *Gospel Series in Spiritual Science*. It should also be noted that Ferne Anderson brought clarity and understanding to Emma's life and teachings through her Master's Thesis at the University of Denver.

Now, we can add Michael Terranova's name to this list. Because of his devotion to her writings and his determination that they be continually available to a broader audience, we have this beautiful new edition, *Class Lessons of 1888*. Thank you, Michael, for the wonderful service you have provided for a whole new generation of Emma students.

Emma Curtis Hopkins was known as the "teacher of teachers." Here's what her student, Rev. Charles Fillmore, the founder of the Unity Church movement, had to say about her:

> "She is undoubtedly the most successful teacher in the world. In many instances those who enter her classes confirmed invalids come out at the end of the course perfectly well. Her very presence heals and those who listen are filled with new life. Never before on this planet have such words of burning Truth been so eloquently spoken through a woman."

I wholly concur.

May the love and wisdom that Emma expresses through her writings reach into your soul and bless your life.

*Rev. Marcia Sutton*
*Milwaukie, Oregon,*
*November 2005*

# Introduction

My first introduction to Emma Curtis Hopkins was the study of *High Mysticism* in 1964. This was followed by *Gospel Series in Spiritual Science* and the *Bible Interpretations*. In 1990 I was asked to take over the direction of the home study courses at the Sanctuary of Truth in Alhambra, an international program for the study of Mrs. Hopkins' writings. During that time I wrote study guides and taught classes on Mrs. Hopkins' life and works.

Emma Curtis Hopkins was born when the new country of America was beginning to question the beliefs and values of the Old World. While Europe was steeped in its history and rigid traditions, in America, new ideas, and a "New Thought," were coming into being with a deliberately optimistic message of possibility and hope to set us free from ideas of fear, sin, despair, and punishment. It was a wondrous ferment of ideas, from such thinkers as Phineas Parkhurst Quimby, Ralph Waldo Emerson, Mary Baker Eddy, and the poets Henry David Thoreau and Walt Whitman.

Emma was profoundly influenced by the tremendous philosophical richness into which she was born. She was very well educated, as were both of her parents. At an early age she read the classics in their original Latin and Greek. She was also familiar with the *Bhagavad Gita*, and the *Zend Avesta* of Zoroaster, along with the world's great philosophers and saints. Her wide scholarship in spiritual writings gave her unique insight into the metaphysical interpretation of the Bible and helped her clarify its doctrine of the Christ Principle of Truth.

She acknowledged three Sciences:

Material Science declares laws that are sure: as iron sharpeneth iron, and hydrogen and oxygen clashing together fall into thirst-quenching water; Mental Science to which the world can subscribe, as "All that we are is made up of our thought;' and Mystical Science which announces the miracles of 'Predicateless Being' setting the ways of matter at naught, and nullifying the thoughts of mind.

First-time readers may find her poetic language difficult to follow, but they should not be put off by this. She was writing in the richly expressive English language of 17th-century King James, still in use in the late 19th century. Her evocative presentation of Truth principles gives a clear grasp of spiritual ideas and brings them to life, for, after all, they are to be *lived.*

Today, in the 21st Century, we are again in a ferment of ideas as science and religion, physics and metaphysics attempt to understand one another. How fortunate we are to have the ancient teachings Mrs. Hopkins has woven into her writings to guide us in today's world—for what we call "New Thought" is actually the wisdom of the ages.

*Rev. Shirley Lawrence, Director*
*Emma Curtis Hopkins Studies Program*
*Sanctuary of Truth*
*South Pasadena, California*

# THE LESSONS

# LESSON ONE

## In the Beginning God Created

All study of mind or mental action or phenomena is essentially metaphysical, taking the student above or out of the province or range of pure physics, which deals with visible phenomena and their laws.

Thus the study of mind and its laws of operation has been called the study of metaphysics, and the knowledge obtained, classified and arranged for further systematic investigation, may be properly termed mental or metaphysical science.

When but partially understood, or known only in its partial application, simply for the cure of bodily ailments, the practice of mind for such results has been called "mind cure," meaning that by the use of mind in some way or other, bodily infirmities and maladies could be healed, as formerly water was used for such purposes, and all practice with that agent was called "water cure."

In school metaphysics or mental science, the study seems to have been for the most part a record of the phenomena of cerebration, as conscious and unconscious, cognitive and motive, without definite information as to whether mental action, controllable or uncontrollable, could be held responsible for health and disease.

The other extreme, taken by those unacquainted with school metaphysics, is that mind is useful mainly as a curative agent for bodily sickness.

But mental science has three departments of application to the wants and needs of the people:

1. Therapeutic — Which treats of mind in its relation to all bodily conditions. Shows how health and disease are the results of thought, and teaches such rules of thought as will change physical infirmities of all kinds, as deformity, disease, sickness, weakness, pain, and even liability to all these, to a state of health and exemption from danger of their recurrence.

2. Ethical — Which treats of the relation of habitual thought to character quality and intellectual faculty. Uplifts life motives and renovates morals. Intensifies the powers of intellect, and turns the attention of students from sordid cares and depressing anxieties to peace and freedom of mind. It is practical application and proof of the old Socratic doctrine that men act wrongly because they form erroneous judgments. It teaches the laws and conditions upon which right thinking depends, or such thinking as regulates character, conduct and judgment.

3. Religious — Which treats of the nature of mind, soul and spirit. Shows them to be identical in essence. Proves every mind — every soul to be the direct offspring and emanation of the Divine Soul or Mind and teaches the rebinding of the soul of man to the All-Soul or Divine Soul after the supposed disjunctive agency of sin is annulled. (Religion, from *re* and *lige*). It is practical revival of the doctrine: "I and my Father are one"-"That they may be one with me as I am one with thee" — "ye are the sons of the Most High," which is the most ancient spiritual teaching known to the race.

Each department closely relates to the other, and in explaining and defining each, the other is broadly intimated or taught.

The Therapeutic application of mind claims attention most strenuously as yet, and all instruction in the new metaphysics is devoted more especially to healing of bodily sicknesses, brain affections, or whatever infirmities the flesh claims. It is promising evidence of the advance of the Science into the higher thought of the people to find that latterly many have urged: Why devote so potent a reformatory principle to the simple healing from physical maladies, when moral and religious instructions have fallen so far short of their high mission? Why not bend the energies of scientific discovery to the curing of depraved tastes and vicious lives?

Formerly the complaint was against the broad claims of the science of metaphysics, going as it did so far as to invade religion and ethics, and its simple disciples were haughtily bidden to stick to their physical healing, leaving religion to the wise clergy whose preaching and doctrines stimulate intelligence and rouse hope.

To the scorn of the past or the reproof of the present the trained scientist is indifferent, keeping on her steadfast way, helping, encouraging, healing everywhere, knowing that in process of time all good will come to the people through the law she is practicing.

All who come before classes for the study of the science are miracles of proof of its mighty efficiency in some one or other application of its laws. There are those who were once hopeless and despairing invalids, with diseased bodies they prayed to be rid of, now healthy and joyous people teaching the way others like them may be saved out of their bondage.

Others tell of salvation from worse bondage than disease — slavery to depraved tastes and evil propensities. They also are teaching the law of holy living and righteous thinking, to the joy and uplifting of all who will hear.

There are many who tell how close creeds and cramping theological beliefs had dwarfed mental growth and spiritual unfolding 'til life was a perpetual siege and battle of resentment against the dealings of the Great Invisible Being who had decreed such merciless laws of life. When such are set free, they seem the fulfillment of certain prophecies of old, that when Truth shall be preached in the latter days the mouths of the dumb shall be opened and the tongues of them that cannot speak shall be eloquent in its praise, "that its way may be known upon all the earth, its saving health among the nations."

Now all these results are reached by methods differing in most important and vital particulars from the recognized systems, religious, educational and medical, that have ruled the world study and practice hitherto.

We find people bring about moral changes and bodily renovations, who knew nothing of past or present theories of medication, who had no traditional knowledge of a single one of the 265 curative drugs handed down from Hippocrates to the learned in pharmaceutic art of our own time, or of the anatomy of the human body, though the same old naming and description have instructed generation after generation since the days of Herophilus of Alexandria (who dissected criminals alive for surgical enlightenment).

People who could not preach a sermon on the nature of the soul, who had no theories of the effect of social life and morals on individual life, or of individual life on social currents at large, have been found accomplishing works of healing and moral changes far outstripping the performances of the learned in medical sciences and surgery, the temperance workers, "White Cross" legions, moral education promoters and missionary societies' endeavors.

It is generally known to investigators, and particularly known to the best practitioners, that all the most miraculous results are produced without visible aids, appliances, applications, restoratives, touch of hands or material remedies whatsoever; and in cases of moral cure, without pleading, preaching, urging or threatening on the part of the worker. But all changes are wrought by and in the mysterious silence of the scientific worker's secret mind.

Insofar as visible helps are resorted to, the practitioner of healing nowadays shows ignorance of the inherent powers of mind to do all healing, and ignorance of the science of mind whose knowledge makes other restorative agencies prove themselves ridiculous.

The earnestness and eagerness with which all classes of people seize upon the study, whether they scold or condemn the "so-called science," or whether they believe in and practice it, only shows the perpetual effort of the race to get wholeness — to solve the problem of life by looking into all that pertains to life conditions. The quest of life is satisfaction. This is the one word that expresses the whole effort of life in everything that lives.

How to get satisfaction is the problem that absorbs the attention of the race. It has absorbed the attention of all races in all ages. Those who set out on the search for health are pursuing one branch of the great problem of wholeness or satisfaction.

The definition of satisfaction is conceded to be, peace of mind, knowledge of absolute truth, and health of body.

These sides of the triangle satisfaction cover all the ground of all the desires of the human heart. All religions and sciences have for their foundation or underlying intention, the teaching of the race so to live as to bring that threefold answer. They have all failed; totally failed. There is great running to and fro among us; people's hearts failing them — doubting and fearing each other, even them of their own households, but most of all doubting and fearing the great Force that drives cyclones, lowers lightning flashes, shakes mountain fastnesses and separates loved ones.

Nobody is sure that any knowledge he has obtained from intricate calculations and laborious researches is Truth; that with all his computations and measurements he knows even the orbits of the planets; or that with all his spectrum analyses he can tell the constitution and color of the sun. "The most that we know is that we know nothing," say the wisest materialists. Neither are they sure which of all the teachings of pulpit, itinerant preacher, or missionary is the one safe for all to follow — Jew and Christian, civilized and heathen — since the doctrine of each, obeyed to the letter, has made its devotees intolerant and cruel, slaughtered men like sheep, and desolated countless hearts.

Where is the health that has been sought with universal scramble? With all our knowledge of witty inventions, cruel dissections and vivisections, microscopic investigations and surgical proficiency, diseases have multiplied and universal sickness devastates our homes. So much for ages of effort to solve the problem of life and get its true answer, Satisfaction.

Note that the results of a practical knowledge of mental science or metaphysics are identical with what is conceded to be the threefold condition which the true solution of the problem of life must show — awakened intelligence, purified morals, bodily health. Thus the life problem and the health problem would seem to be identical, and the principle of life and health one and the same.

All work accomplished by the mental scientist or metaphysician, has its foundation in a knowledge of just this truth, and the measure of the excellence of his work is the measure of his understanding of this principle. The inability to define or explain his basis in principle has been the occasion of the criticism and ridicule hurled at him by press, pulpit and logician. And even when ardent students have named the foundation statement that their argumentation springs from, they have not been listened to by reason of the fact that many cures are wrought by apparently inferior or imperfect characters.

"You need not tell by their titles what books you have read. (I infer your reading from the wealth and accuracy of your conversation.)" If these critics had well read a certain ancient classic author, they would have found recognized cause why inferior or imperfect mentalities may cure physical disorders by the use of mental action. "The thought of every mind is a likeness of that mind and imprints itself upon every other mind, making others more like the mind that sends the strong thought forth." Many a thinker of bodily health is a forgetter of moral excellence, and in sending his quality forth makes the recipient of his thought, like himself, a forgetter of justice and charity, even while he builds for him — temporarily — a robust body.

"We must never say, I do not know this, therefore, it is false. We must study to know, know to understand, and understand in order to judge." When one knows, understands and truly judges, he finds that health, happiness and outward circumstances are well or ill with us according as we have thought falsely or truly of the problem of life. It is the principle involved in this which must be understood, before intelligent discussion of merits can be entered into respecting the reasonableness or folly of the claims of mental students. It takes certain knowledge of mathematical principles before the demonstrations of the geometrician are intelligible. Science is science, and whether it is a problem in health or mathematics we are solving, we must know the principle involved or be liable to misjudgment and failure.

A problem is a question proposed for solution; something to be worked out. A problem always involves a special principle or principles which must be stated before propositions can be reasonably combined to bring forth a result proving the soundness of the principle stated.

The problem of life has not been solved by any of us. Each one tells his neighbor that his life has turned out all wrong in spite of his efforts to solve it according to the plan he has laid down. No system as taught, has given us such a hold on the laws of life as to bring to us peace of mind, certain conviction of what is truth, and health of body.

While supposing that satisfaction lies along certain lines we think we must pursue them. But satisfaction does not come, though we have struggled along the path pointed out by the wisest of our teachers. Under the pressure of desire and surrounding temptations we do the best we can, but only to fail. We have a dim consciousness that we are continually in error — "prone to err as the sparks fly upward." So much light as to know we are perpetually wrong we have, but the way to do exactly right is hid. "Why is light given to a man whose way is hid?"

"Is there a solution of this problem, or is there not?" the people are asking. "If there is, show it to us, you to whom we have paid tithes of mint, anise and cumin of gold, honors and opportunities to find its way for us — if not, sound the alarm from lip to lip the world over, for man is betrayed!"

When little children find the results of their calculation altogether wrong, they go back to the beginning of their problem, state the principle to be demonstrated, announce the propositions and apply their rules.

Let us become like little children with the problem we have got so fearfully wrong.

As it is the problem of life we are discussing, the principle involved must be the Life Principle. A study of the Life Principle must be a study of beginning, creation, origin, cause.

Now whether we have prejudice for or against the disciples of a system, if we would study the system fairly we must set the prejudice aside. Whether we favor the character and conduct of the men whose historic connection with Bible doctrines has necessitated their figuring in that book or not, we cannot, in studying origin, ignore an authority on the subject which has been respected by many wise students of life in all ages, and which so boldly states, without excuse or apology, as if unquestionably true and accurate, a certain proceeding called the creation of earth and all living things. This authority is said to be the written statement of Eadras, indited by him in a mood of what he called intuitional memory of the oral teachings of the Hebrew law-giver, Moses.

The teachings are almost identical with those of all real students of life and its laws in all times. Wherever taught or recorded they have been called sacred truths and carefully cherished as the wisdom of the devout and learned in life's mysteries. The remarkable analogies of the Christian Bible and Hindu Sacred Books, Egyptian Ancient Teachings, Persian. Bibles, Chinese Great Learning, Oriental Zohar, Saga and many others, show that the whole world has had life teachings so wonderfully identical as to make them all subjects for respectful attention and investigation by the thoughtful of our age.

"In the beginning God created." They all say this.

Was the writer speaking of the time of an actual beginning? No, in principle *creative Deus* has no reference to time. To one who searches in most meanings these words tell that *in the great forever without beginning of years or end of days God is creating, or creates.*

The responsible center of the statement is the word God, whose name in all languages is THE GOOD. The Good is creating. "Thou great First Cause, least understood."

*Deus est omnium rerum causa, immanens non transiens.*[1] A creator — not the "Great Absentee of the Universe," who having set the mysterious mechanism into action left it to spin its desolate way unheeded — but the perpetual causation of all things; the responsible center of all life. His name is *The Good.*

What and where is *The Good?* Life is good. There is no point of space or place where Life as Life is not good. If one says life is not good, he does not mean that Life as Life is not good, but only that his experience with conditions is unendurable. Life is good, and Good is God; thus God is Life. There is no point of space or place where Life is

---

[1] "God is the cause of all things, immanent not changing."

not Good — thus Life is Omnipresence. "There is only one Life in the universe."

Truth is Good. There is no point of space or place where truth is not Good. And Good is God. Thus God is Truth. "Burn the libraries, said Omar, "for their value is in the Koran;" and the Koran says, "God is Truth." Plato only is entitled to the statement of Omar, says a great teacher of ethics, for he tells what all wise men teach. "Out of Plato come all things that are still written and debated among men." And Plato says, "God is Truth." "Truth is Lord of all, and there is nothing higher than it," teaches the oldest religious philosophy of the world.

Love is Good. There is no point of space or place where Love as Love is not Good. If one says that Love is not good he does not mean Love as Love, but only that his desires toward a certain object are unbearable — his selfish terror lest there be no adequate return of affection is unendurable. This is not Love. Love is Good; and Good is God. Thus God is Love.

Substance is Good. That upon which we can rely — depend. That which stands under, sustains, upholds. If reliable and dependable, then unchangeable, steadfast, immutable, indestructible, unfailing, eternal. If unchangeable, reliable, steadfast, eternal, then essentially opposite in character, office and name from that which has been termed substance — the changing, temporal, unreliable matter of the physical world. And if opposite in name, character and office, to matter, then Spirit is the substance that is good, occupying all space and all place. Spirit is Good; and Good is God. Thus "God is Spirit." (Right rendering of John IV. 24). "God is the only Substance."

Intelligence is Good. There is no point of space or place where Intelligence is not Good. Intelligence is Mind which to be Good must be steadfast, reliable, unchangeable, unfailing, eternal. Thus Intelligence as Good is Mind, steadfast, eternal. Mind is Good; and Good is God; thus God is Mind. The Omnipresence, First Cause, Creative Principle. The only Substance in all the universe. The only Deity. The only God. The Good. "Thou shalt have no other gods before me." That other deity set up — whose name is Evil — the origin and governing law of all evil conditions — has no space or place or where — no kingdom — no subjects, no substance, no reality. To believe in

9

such a governing force and law-giver is to do homage to another deity besides The Good. Idolatry is the worship or acknowledgment of a false God! Who are idolaters?

All devout teachers of Truth have said that from the Only Life all Life proceeds. From the Only Mind all mind emanates. By so dealing with the problem of Life, we find this statement of a principle commonly accepted by all; The First Cause is Mind. Thus given the mind of man and the Mind that is God identical, how shall we think so as to prove it? Given, the life of man and the Life that is identical, how live so as to prove it. "Heirs of God and joint heirs with Christ." "Offspring of the Most High."

We have been working at the problem of life with two opposing Creators, proposing the mind of man and the Mind that is God different and opposed. How could we think so as to get into harmony with the Good? Given the life of man and the life that is God different and opposed, how live so as to be reconciled to Life?

# LESSON TWO

## Truth Shall Make You Free

It is written that the Truth shall make us free, as if Truth were a mysterious working principle, capable of accomplishing our salvation from evil and danger. As if the statement of it, if it could be actually known what Truth is, were all that is necessary to lift us out of bondage.

Either the statement is true or it is false. If it is true, it can be proved and will do the work. If false it will not prove, and we shall grope on in the old darkness, knowing not the way out of our bondage.

All are under bondage to something. "Every heart knoweth its own bitterness," — that which it is under bondage to. One suffers the pangs of a guilty conscience, a fearful load. Perhaps cruelty to wife or children or parents haunts him. Maybe he has wronged and cheated his fellow-man. Or some secret sin makes him ashamed before himself and afraid to be left alone with the silence. Some are under the bondage of weakness and deformity. To some, wasting sickness and gnawing disease render life that might be sweet and full, a burden and time of groaning. Some have lost beloved companions and see the vista of years stretch ahead, with only the memory of past joys; no hope, no satisfaction with new friends possible, — only loneliness on and on. Death has been the terror and cruel monster of their lives. They are among the beaten, the worse than death — the desertion of loved ones; no burden heavier. Who shall deliver them from "the body of this death!"

Some carry the weight of discouragement because of the failure of every plan and effort of their lives. They are among the beaten, the thwarted in the battle with life-conditions. Some have found themselves looking upon life-relations with such mistaken judgment that it has seemed to them wisest to deceive family, neighbors, friends, the world, respecting themselves, their motives, their possessions, their work; and the weight of the gigantic fraud of their own lives, even themselves cannot calculate. A terrible burden is mistaken judgment.

Now the Truth, it is written, will set us free from all the bondage under which we suffer — the bondage of evil. What evil? Sin, sickness, death. All the evils we know are included under these three heads.

In seeking for freedom from bondage, then, we are seeking for Truth. The search for freedom from disease is the one-sided or partial effort to get absolute Truth, because only absolute Truth will set absolutely free. Absolute Truth is Universal Truth. Only Universal Truth will set all people free. If one religious band says slavery and polygamy are good, and, being more powerful than the poor heathen and simple woman, they take them into bondage, then what they say is not Universal Truth, for Universal Truth makes universal freedom. Part of the people are in bondage under their statement, so it is not universal or absolute Truth.

The eager rush of all, the solemn despair of the thoughtful, who, after ages of seeking cry, "What does it all amount to? Life is not worth living if we cannot get hold of the right solution to our problem," seem to indicate that there must be a way out of the sorrow and sin of people.

If the Truth does make free when taught — free from evil — and if we are all under evil still, then we do not yet know Truth. Not to know is ignorance. Then ignorance of Truth is cause of evil. Gautama Buddha, a tender and compassionate teacher of life, being sorrowful over the miseries of the creatures of earth, sought long and earnestly to find the cause of so much sorrow, anguish and despair. He wept and fasted and lay in the dust of abjectest humility before the Unseen Presence, whatever its name might be, to inquire what the cause. And when he had got down to the bedrock of sincerest humiliation, where himself was forgotten, and one with the Intelligence which alone could answer him, he heard a voice saying, "Ignorance of Truth is the cause of the misery. Teach them Truth; and the Truth shall make them free." Then he arose and went about seeking Truth — that Truth which should be freedom for every creature.

Oh! What is Truth and where shall it be found?

There was one teacher of life and its duties — wise, compassionate, and tender he was — who came among men, bringing the laws of health, of joy, of wholesome satisfaction; and he said that the accepted written Scriptures were good testimony to the excellence of his system. Deep searching into their meanings, thereby discovering their hidden sense, would reveal to all the ways of life and peace. "Search the Scriptures, for in them ye think ye have eternal life; and they are they which testify of me."

Eternal life to the people to whom he spoke was the sum of heavenly bestowal; it meant all the joys of the blest. There is a living, breathing joy, in knowing Truth, they said, that causes those who know it to cry, "My words are life to them that find them, and health to all their flesh."

To search the Scriptures for Truth seems to be the only way for us, for the wisest students of nature and human experience agree that the most they know is that they know nothing; so from all their schemes we can hope no good. Now, the Scriptures say, "To be carnally minded is death, but to be spiritually minded is life and peace." One set of Scriptures says that the enemy of spirituality is materiality. Hence, if we would get the seeing eye and hearing ear with respect to divine things, we must dematerialize ourselves. Thus we find knowledge of Truth, and being spiritually minded, identical.

There is a thought that has run like a golden thread through the noisy wars and quarrelings of nations. Kingdoms have risen and fallen; philosophies have sunk into disrepute; the conclusions of geologist, astronomer, and religionist are the rubbish of the past but this thought has run along in the hearts of the wise among all peoples, told in almost the same language, as, "Truth being one, its language must be one, and they who speak Truth must say the same things." This deathless thought of the wise has been, "That there is a *divine idea* pervading the outward and visible universe, which outward and visible universe is but the shadow, the sign, the symbol of the idea, having in itself no reality, no meaning apart from the idea. To the mass of mankind the idea is hidden; but to seize upon the idea which each outward thing signifies, would be to all men a good condition of life, and health, and peace, and the end of all spiritual effort for all ages. How should we seize hold upon the idea? With the mind only.

The result of seizing the idea which material things signify, agrees exactly with the saving outcome of being spiritually minded and knowing Truth. That is, life, and health and peace.

Thus in searching for health we really are seeking to be spiritually minded. If we do not know that which brings health, we are not the spiritually minded. It makes no difference how much we know, it is knowledge that profiteth not, if knowing it has for its answer, "The most we know is that we know nothing," and death is on the increase. If we have not learned to carry health and freedom by the words of our lips, we are far from carrying the signs of true knowledge.

Notice that sin, sickness and sorrow are laid at the doors of ignorance. And ignorance is a state of the mind. Health, righteousness and joy are the fruits of true knowledge — understanding. And understanding is a state of the mind, making all good and all evil to mankind to lie in right or wrong states of mind.

All the systems of the world have taught us the direct opposite of the ways that lead to life and health and peace. They have not taught us to be spiritually minded. Where, if we desire health and peace, shall we look for the way that will bring them? The Scriptures are said to teach the way. But only the right interpretation of them will lead us into it. "Search!" Searching implies deep looking. Deeper looking than anybody has yet done, it seems, for its wisest students are far from peace and true living.

We begin very meekly to search the Scriptures of all languages. We find that they all teach there is but one substance in the universe. We find that the great convocation of clergy were right in concluding that in the written Scripture, material terms are used to convey great spiritual truths, and physical transactions, descriptions and namings should have metaphysical interpretations.

We find that there is a great truth underlying the symbology taught by the ancients. Those who have studied these laws in any measure are not so startled at being told that all Scripture is written in symbolism, and only by the right interpretation of the terms and namings used therein, can the true meanings be found. Upon knowing this, some will remember how it has been taught, that to know the deep-most meaning of written Scripture, would be to know the laws of life and spiritual unfolding. It is the living hidden meaning within it that has kept it alive in the teeth of skepticism, materialism, and "scientific opposition" of all kinds, through the ages.

Deep searching reveals these hidden meanings. It teaches that one law of natural phenomena, observed by the students of nature, is the law by which mind goes from ignorance of truth to knowledge of truth. It is the law of sameness of procedure, whereby to know the ongoing of one living thing, from proto-plasmic void and uselessness to time of fruiting or usefulness, is to know the history of all things. Natural science teaches that the protoplasm of insect, beast, man, is indistinguishable in kind, and the stages of progress toward perfect unfolding are identical in all. The phenomena of nature symbolize and hint the unfolding of mind from ignorance to understanding.

From dark planted seed to fruiting time,

we the symbol and type of our destiny see.

The earth itself in all its movements symbolizes mind. "The earth was without form and void, and darkness was upon the face of the deep, and the spirit of God moved upon the face of the waters, and God said, "Let there be light." The awakening of the slumbering energies of wisdom that lie dormant in the mind, is pictured by that statement. Darkness is a symbol of ignorance, and light is a symbol of knowledge. Spirit is but another name for word, as "My words are spirit;" and "Waters" is the symbolic word for mind acting consciously, or conscious mind. The word moves upon the face of the waters: "Let there be light." As if the earth must do something of her own initial faculty — put forth her own effort to rift the dark clouds and slumbering shadows, and let the light shine over her. It is to us a lesson.

We are in the darkness and cloud of ignorance. It makes no difference if we call our ignorance knowledge; if we are not free, it is clouds of ignorance. We have many beliefs; if they are not health they are false beliefs. We must get rid of them. By this it would seem that ignorance were made up of false beliefs.

Deep searching reveals that the Scriptures teach the scheme of life to be freedom from bondage, and perfect freedom is knowledge of Truth. "If any man will come after me (follow Truth), let him deny himself," — deny himself as he seems, all his folly and foolishness, all his ignorance, all his false old beliefs. Now if ignorance means false beliefs and folly, it is high time we were denying them if denying them will bring us into line with Truth.

What are the false beliefs which make up the sum total of our ignorance? The Scriptures show that we have five false beliefs in common, which we must deny if we would be free. As there were five porches between the lame man and the beautiful waters of healing, so there are five strong guards of false beliefs between the waiting mind and the healing baptism of Truth. What are these false beliefs, and how shall we deny them?

**1. The Race has believed in more than one governing Force and Law Giver for the Universe, in spite of saying, by occasional declarations and counter-statements, that there is but one, who occupies all space and place, whose name is The Good. The race believes that there is a principle operating in the universe against the Good; its dominion over the world is so great, "from the river to the uttermost seas," that one of Boston's ablest clergymen said, that sometimes he believed "evil to be a greater power than good."**

Now, if the universally conceded statement be true, viz.: that there is one Force omnipresently acting, which is Deity, or God, whose name is *The Good*, then that belief that there is another force acting besides it, is a false belief.

Then we must deny it. How shall we deny it? There is but one way under heaven: take the belief by name and give it the lie. *There is no evil.* Go ye into all the world with this word. Now if the Truth makes free when it is spoken, then if that is Truth, the result of speaking it should be freedom from evil. Is it? Try it.

Knowing *why* there is but One Principle governing the universe, send your strong, vehement thought out over the invisible air to speed like an arrow straight on its mission. Do you know the nature of a thought — that it is deathless, indestructible, invisible arrow, charged with the kind of mind you have, and strikes out into other minds to change them to be more like you? Wherever this thought strikes, that there is no principle of evil operating against the Only Power in the universe; cruelty and greed and crime die away like echoes in the wake of your true word. They *ought* to, if what you say is true, for it is written that "the truth makes free."

Some hard closing grasp of unendurable circumstance, sorrow in the home, injustice and oppressive dealings, vanish, fall away as dreams of the night from the broken heart and hopeless life where your word goes. They flee from your own life also. How can they help fleeing if you speak the Truth? Not something you have done, but something you have said, a Principle that has been made known to you, has set you free. "He doeth the works." Truth is a silent Principle, waiting in its vastness of silence through the ages for words to set it into manifest action. Thou shalt have no other Deity but one, "Turn and acknowledge Me."

> 2. The race believes in more than one substance in the universe, and that it has a visible presence, a name, and way of working. Now if there is but one Presence, one Force, one Substance, that belief of another substance than the One, the omnipresent Spirit, is a false belief, and stands for rejection or denial. *There is no matter.* Hurl the belief from the weighted mind. If it is true that there is no matter, you will be free from matter and its way of working. To those who have spoken these words, these results have come: the hard tumor, the stiffened joint relax.

Where has the close grip gone that held the pitiful limb prisoner? Where has the lie gone that built the unreal, untrue picture? Matter becomes plastic to the strong vehement word of Truth. I pray you speak it. Let the walls of your prison house be a hundred feet thick, and your swift word shall fly through the night to the judge and law readers, to harass them till they find the saving clause, or move the people to set you free; some angel by night to open your prison doors, as the Apostles of old were set free. "Enter the path."

3. The race has given the name, character and excellence of Deity, to what has no reality; — to the non-being and substanceless, the name Substance; to the lifeless, the name Life; to the non-intelligent, the name Intelligence. The race has believed that there is Life, Substance and Intelligence in matter. The belief is found under the light of argument from a certain premise to be a false belief. It stands for denial. Give it the lie. There is no Life, Substance, or Intelligence in matter. Material life, substance and seeming intelligence should fade and fail if that be Truth.

Speak the words. Those who have spoken them tell us that the whole world changes to them as the objects of nature change to our view when the light shines over them after the night. Some who have hoped great things from earth-life, finding, as all must sooner or later, all its blessings temporal, elusive, sitting under the roof-tree of desolation, the shadow of disappointment, lift eyes to the invisible heavens and cry with a new joy, "I know that my Redeemer liveth. I will not mourn, I know that the Comforter cometh. 'He shall deliver me in six troubles — yea, in seven there shall no evil touch me.' "

One who has lived, believing the riches, profits and advantages of material transactions are worthwhile, feels suddenly the vainglory of them, and forgetting to calculate upon them, cries, "Vanity of vanities! " or, lying in the midst of all his splendor, means, "I am poorer than the poorest if I do not know of some riches I can take with me — something that will not fail me." He begins to be set free from vanity and sordidness. One who has set great value upon the intelligence stored in the brain; has taken pride in his knowledge of stars and rocks and growing things, begins to realize that "there is a way that seemeth right unto a man but the end thereof are the ways of death," "knowledge that profiteth not." He begins to think what that may mean, "If any man lack wisdom let him ask of God." Ah, none rest till they have sought and found the nameless Wisdom, whose words are health to the inward parts and joy to the fainting heart — the wisdom that age cannot wither nor accident betray.

He sets his feet unto the right way who says, "Life, Substance and Intelligence are Deity Himself — all that claims to be Life and yet dies, Substance and yet decays, Intelligence and yet fails, is but the creation of the imaginations of foolishness, false beliefs which I will not harbor." This one enters into his inheritance of freedom. He must, if it is Truth he speaks, because "The Truth shall make you free."

4. The race believes that the unreal has the faculties of Reality; in other words, that matter sees and hears, and feels. "Thou, God, seest," "He heareth the crying of His children," "We have not a High Priest who cannot be touched with the feeling of our infirmities." Then matter which has no being, no life, no intelligence, how can it have the sensations of Mind, Soul, Spirit? *There is no sensation in matter.* One speaks this great word out over the waiting universe. He who has set great store by the physical body, which is like a shadow that declineth, loses his taste for the pleasures of sense; false appetites fall away, "What shall it profit me," he says, "if I gain the whole world and lose my Soul?" Somebody, moaning on couch of pain, lifts his head and cries, "I am eased of my pain."

5. The race believes that in a universe created by The Good, governed and occupied by The Good, there is sin, sickness, and death. "We miscreate our own evils." "All that we see is the result of what we have thought." Deny the false belief, saying earnestly, "There is no reality in these things, *There is no sin, sickness or death.*" These words are true and true results follow. The hand lifted to strike falls powerless. Some selfish grasp of the powerful upon the labor and against the rights of the feeble, relaxes. The weapon raised to injure finds the motive that prompted it die into indifference. Some cruel deed thought in the heart hurries out and away to die in the shame of forgetful-

ness. Some heart, terrified by all these, feeling the rush of the white wings of Truth, lifts his unconquerable spirit to the heavens and sings, "I will fear no evil, for Thou art with me." Instead of the lie that struggled to utter itself, a sweet truth springs to the lips. The heart that was filled with unbelief, begins to trust in God.

> The healing of Truth's seamless dress
>
> Moves past sick beds and pain;
>
> We touch it in life's throng and press,
>
> And are made whole again.

The dying feel the living Truth stir every fiber to new leases of life. "The Truth shall make you free." Free from what? Free from evil. What is evil? Sin, sickness, death; we do not know any other evils but these.

The ancients tried a system of denials; they mortified the body with torture and fasting, neglect and cold, going without shelter and raiment, to teach sensation that it had no rights, and will that it had all. The asceticism of the early religionists taught days of fasting and abstinence from bodily comforts, to teach the nothingness of the earthly man — the flesh that is as grass. To deny the world, the flesh and the devil; to put behind, as temptations of Satan, all earthly comforts — thus was the law of true denial hinted at. The teachers of ethics showed how "only with renunciation, life, properly speaking, begins." "Not till we have learned to expect nothing, do we compel all things to our service." "Fly the boundaries of the senses, live the ideal life freed thought can give." How eagerly they sought the five denials of the science of life.

> Many a house of life hath held me
>
> Seeking ever that which wrought
>
> This prison of the senses, sorrow-fraught.
>
> Sore was my ceaseless strife.
>
> But now, thou builder of this tabernacle,

Now I know thee who thou art.

Never shalt thou build again these walls of pain,

Nor raise the roof-trees of deceit.

Nor lay fresh rafters on the clay.

Broken thy house is, and the ridge-pole split;

Delusion fashioned it.

Sage pass I thence, deliverance to obtain.

# LESSON THREE

## Courage to Go On

Perhaps nothing strikes the young student of science with more dismay than to find so many of the people who have learned it, still suffering from attacks of bodily illness, still having disease and death in the family, unable to cure their cases and exhibiting signs of their old sinfulness just as plainly as other people.

It suddenly occurs to the beginner that the science cannot do all that is claimed for it; that "there must be limits to its power over the life, character and work of its advocates."

And so it does look at first sight. Can there be a reasonable explanation that will give us courage to go on?

Let us see.

Every mind, taking up the science, is shrouded in the darkness of false beliefs that must of necessity show forth as false conditions. False conditions are the not-good conditions, whether pride and meanness of character, or neuralgia of the face. False beliefs are false states of the mind — clouds of darkness, making the mind unfit to send forth curing thoughts for the body, or cleansing thoughts for the character. They must be thrown out of or off the mind before the conditions will be right.

How are they to be thrown out? There is only one way under heaven to clear the mind of its errors and that is to take each error in turn, call it by name, and declare that it has no reality in it. Few minds can be found willing to do this. Every mind, almost without exception, desires to make cures and bring forth great results without having been cleared of its old beliefs; and expects to have the arguments for

23

healing given to it along with the old thoughts, no matter what they are, and to be able to use them at once as effectively as does one who has been scientifically faithful.

It is impossible to look except with amazement upon certain students who at first set out with faithful rejection of the beliefs they had held, and while faithful were able to bring forth healing fruits; but who, after a while, have grown tired of the rigor of the law, and have let the same old errors come creeping back to rest like clouds upon the hills, or fogs in the valleys of mind — worldly ambitions, intolerance of other people's rights, or other countless errors. Then the healing thoughts, which only come forth from the mind that is willing to be trained, no longer sound reasonable, no longer have potency, and these people complain bitterly of the science, and cannot be counted in with real scientists while they remain in this unscientific state.

All the time we are met by these people — people who are cruel in their treatment of others, people who are sharp in money dealings, people who talk one way and do another, people who are sick, or lame, or infirm. None of these have yet cleared their mind of personal beliefs in the reality of some of these things that science calls false. Too much stress cannot be put upon the imperative necessity of getting our own mind true, before we can be sure of bringing forth the truest results to others.

Thou must be true thyself if thou the truth would'st teach,

Thy soul must overflow with truth, the truth results to reach.

Then the time that it takes to heal — to get the character true; the science is also blamed for this, and called inefficient, when the real reason is that the mind has not done anything for its own training into excellence — its own salvation. Time is no factor to the clean mind; "the twinkling of an eye." But the mind must first be cleansed. Some students are discouraged and impatient at the outset, because they cannot have the arguments for healing given them at the very first lesson. But seeds will not spring up to perfect fruitage till the arid soil has been enriched and irrigated and suited to their growth. So thoughts will not be "healing for the nations" till the mind that sends them forth is trained to strength and certainty. The arguments for healing used by the unscientific mind soon bring it to a dead standstill.

We should take courage by knowing that the very worst of these minds will be changed to excellence by faithful effort.

When told that these steps of treatment of, or teaching, the principles upon which the healing practice is based, are the scientific explanation of the doctrines and miracles of Christ and his Apostles, of course the questioner is on the alert instantly, and willing to investigate the science — especially the mind that insists upon a foundation in reason for every practice it undertakes.

The word *science* is the rallying cry in every department of effort and line of pursuit. This is the age of investigation of phenomena, and their relations to the wants and affairs of the people. It is conceded that when the science of it is mastered, or that which details the practical workings of a principle, and explains how to set it into action, even prayer-cure may be explained, and understood, and that everybody praying according to law might find answer according to law, just as every skillful manipulator for the keys of the electric machine is master of the subtle fluid itself. Thus, the process known, the principle is revealed.

Certain students of health-laws, while searching and experimenting, found that the mind trained to certain ways of thinking would bring health of body and moral rectitude. Then they began to tell and teach these ways. When their teachings struck the ears of people who had taken the testimony of sensation for absolute truth, or who had believed that the eyes, ears, and hands report truly, they were shocked. They went about saying that the statements were preposterous. "No evil!" they exclaimed. "What are we to do with murderers and thieves, and the cruel tempered?" They pointed to statistics of crime, and mourned over the depravity of the times, and the awful dispensations of providence in the shape of pestilence and plague and troubles sent by the hand of their God.

It is as if a teacher should sit down in despair upon seeing on a blackboard where a class had been working, that every child had called five and five nine. Foolish action; The only way to do is to reject the false conclusion by first saying, "*it is not true, and the whole work is error*"; Then erase it and put down the true conclusion instead.

Science is science; and whether it is a problem in mathematics or life we are solving, the process is the same. Reject the errors, and state what is true. All actions of each individual are out-figurings or out-livings of his supposition that that is the way to get satisfaction, and to answer for himself the problem of his life, so as to bring what he most desires.

The great teachers of law and logic, arts and physics, all declare that though they find wonderful things along their lines of investigation, no results from their studies show how the awful things of evil, that seem more true and real than God himself, can be wiped off the boards of life. They are as sure as their untaught neighbors, that the way of their own life has brought no more actual peace and joy in proportion to the demands they have made, than the commonest labor's way has brought him. They are as far from the goal of their hopes as he.

But the teachers of our science who come before classes now — the practitioners of healing and all workers therein, have the actual record of miraculous performances, either of themselves, or of their co-workers, to which they may point as evidences of the efficiency of the system.

If people who have worked in missions or struggled to Christianize the masses say, when they hear this doctrine, that it is nothing new at all — they have heard or known it all before, every true teacher of science rejoices that he has so much the greater confirmation of his lessons of life.

But surely there must be some difference between the simple statements of sciences, and the old ways of dealing with the same truth when no such practical outcome was reached by them, as follows the words of the way now taught; and they must not be surprised if people following their words and teachings, in the old way, fail to bring the practical homely help that the weary world demands. For the old teachings have been given for centuries with all kinds of variations, but the sick have not been made well, the poor not eased of their sorrow, the unhappy not comforted, except with the promises of help in the far-off future, when "Now! Now!" was the cry.

The world had to be very weary indeed of the recognized systems, before it would listen at all to this science whose students can accomplish the very things the people pray for, for there has always been somebody in every age telling its ways to ears dull of hearing and hearts that would not respond.

The pioneers of the work in this age, all unread in the book lore of the past, did not know that no word of their speaking was really new to the world, that these thoughts have been embalmed in the amber of myth and allegory by the great of old, who have been martyred or made mystic by an unbelieving humanity.

Like flashes of light into dense darkness came some of the special statements that are now used as expressions of faith or belief. In moments of highest realization of Truth they exclaimed, "*There is no reality in evil. There is no matter. There is no SIN! SICKNESS! DEATH!*" These statements struck the ears of a cynical and densely material age, which had concluded only that to be true and real, which it could calculate, weigh and measure. Lens, scales and statistics disputed. The young thinkers could bring no authorities to corroborate or sustain their claims. They did not know that Hermetic philosophy, Chaldean inner laws, the Vedanta, Brahmin tenets and Pythagorean conclusions, could be quoted in their defense. The power of the negation of claims or blank rejection to unformulate the conditions of materiality, whatever they might be, was not suspected to be an old law of secret Eastern practice revived. When they uttered the bold statements, they were threatened with asylums and jails for sophistry and blasphemy. "The natural man perceiveth not the things of the Spirit, and he cannot know them, for they are foolishness unto him."

Paul had said, "There is nothing unclean but to him that thinketh;" to be sure, but that it was a way of stating the formulating power of thought they could not explain. Emerson and Swedenborg had pronounced all evil to be so much negation — non-entity; but while agreeing thus far with Emerson and Swedenborg, they were confused by these great men's contradictions. When they declared no sickness, they did not quote from Hufeland, of the last century who spoke of that region of the being of man which is never sick, and can never be made sick. He knew it to be the only true self — all the rest lie found to be illusion.

When they found that to speak these things in the silence to people, brought to pass the results they desired, they did not know that it was an introduction into Western practice of an ancient Eastern system of instruction. The *guru*, or teacher of the Orient, sits silently in the presence of the *chela* or scholar, and informs him by unvoiced speech, of the secret mysteries he wishes him to understand, and the mind is changed, and the life begins anew.

The people who hear these things now seem to be quite as ignorant, for the most part, of the age and excellence of the methods, as were the unread pioneers of scientific healing; and it seems as if they would verily that the miracles might be wrought by some other less upsetting doctrines and uncanny silence.

When Naaman, the leper Captain of the hosts of Syria, of great renown among the people, wanted to be healed of his leprosy, he rode proudly up in his chariot to Elisha, the prophet of Israel. He was directed to wash seven times in the river Jordan. The simplicity of the prescription angered him. He had supposed the man of God would strike his hand over him, and, with mystic incantic ceremony of magic arts, pronounce the loathsome malady gone. But no; simple obedience to a simple order was all Elisha asked. By and by his under-officers urged him to try the washing. Then he got angry at the River which Elisha recommended; "Are not the rivers Abana and Pharpar, rivers of Damascus, better than the waters of Israel?" he asked. But Jordan was the only river, and seven washings therein the only cleansing efficiency Elisha knew. So great Naaman went down and washed, and low, his flesh became fresh and young like a little child's, ready for strength and growth.

We are all leprous with false belief; livid with the bruises of sorrow, misfortune, loss of loved ones, family discords; rugose from embittered or unchaste thoughts, and we come for healing and saving. If we come seeking the way of health, we come for saving, for heal and save are from the same root in language, and mean the same. "Heal me and I shall be healed; save me and I shall be saved."

The body should be divested of old raiment before new raiment is seemly; the bones of leprous flesh before new flesh is good; the mind of false beliefs before it can take on new ones.

Many who have dealt with the abstruse philosophies and cumbrous theological and political systems of past and present civilizations, come like Naaman, the captain of hosts in his chariot, proudly demanding cure and saving, and scornfully declaring against the absurdity of the simple washing words they must use for the unburdening of their weighted minds.

Were it not for the failure of their systems, the world is so psychologized by the pride of them, that it would not listen to such simple teachings as denial and prayer and trusting, to bring the good and comfort it longs for. But, "I have swept the heavens with my telescope and found no God", says the astronomer; "Shall we sound alarm to a betrayed world?", asked the world-taught traveler; "Diseases have multiplied, and new sicknesses baffle our complicated system of medical guess-work," reports the heir of ages of medical practice.

Science to the pure should be so simple that a child can enter into the understanding of it, and so broad and deep and high that the plummet line of the greatest intellect could never sound its depths, nor the proudest scale its heights. The more simple the mechanism, the greater art in invention, and the more serviceable.

O, the unburdening — the cleansing potency of denials! From leprous scales to blinding cataracts, pain and disease flee their wondrous power.

With the denial of the reality of the material world and fleshly environment, which is the unburdening of our mind of the beliefs that have weighted and darkened it always, comes a sense of airiness and freedom, and the light of knowledge leading to understanding begins to break. But the sense of freedom that comes with voluntarily putting away our beliefs is not understanding. Perfect understanding is wisdom — perfect light. Carried to their highest or ultimate effect upon the mind, life and character, denials give peace — a strange peace — the peace of the Eastern mystic — the Nirvana of the "common" Buddhist, as he himself expresses it.

Made free from delusions and the inward strife —

Quit of the priest and books.

Notice that all schemes for spiritualizing the race have depreciated the teachings of the schools. "Not many wise, not many learned. Not the wisdom of this world, nor of the princes of this world, that come to naught." "Quit of the priests and books." The perfect health scheme is a scheme for spiritualizing the mind.

"Having naught o'er us but the boundless blue," continues the simple child of the still Orient. He would negative away even his identity — lost to responsibility he would be, to realize forever boundlessness and freedom. The child of denial rests — rests.

But then he speaks of another experience; he describes a feeling of desolation that steals over him — blankness — wonder — the long quiet thrills with consciousness. He desires to *know* and *do*. The Eastern practitioner of the science of negation (with rare exceptions) dwells just there, hoping nothing, fearing nothing, his only effort, "to still the desire for identity." This cannot be done. For from the deathless Parent he came forth, of deathless Substance he was made. "Before Abraham was, I am" was not spoken of one alone, but of all the children of the Most High. He gets something of a hint of this, and in bitterness of futile effort, cries,

If any teach Nirvana is to die —

Tell such they lie.

But again, remembering the holy creed he has been taught, he forces himself piously to repeat,

If any teach Nirvana is to live — they lie —

There is no I.

He has lived in the world of sense and has seen how passions and their fruits, sorrow, jealousy, anger, master mankind, and he says, "Life in the senses is not worth living." "If the passions are masters of mankind, if there is no riddance from them but by annihilation, then we will go hence." "The life of the body is evil and a lie, and so the annihilation of that life is a good for which we ought to wish." "To live knowing that suffering, illness, old age and death are inevitable, is not possible; we must get rid of life, get rid of the possibility of living." And having learned the depassioning, dematerializing, desensing power of denial, he sits under the *sal* and banyan all the days of his life denying himself and all things into blankness and utter inefficiency.

But negations have no charm for the forward-impelled, breeze-stirred Westerner. He says, "Life in the senses, with something perpetually to war against, is infinitely preferable to a life of blank uselessness." He studies laws and rules and creeds and tenets; he dominates and dictates and beats and fights against, and trains heart and mind and brain to the grave; and he, too, says, "Life is dead-sea fruit." He externalizes his positive, legislative, and dominating tendency into building of prisons for crime, and reformatories for the poor strugglers with their life-problem none will help them solve, and poorhouses for the fainting wanderers he and his co-legislators have driven from the doors of Truth, the comforting mother. He dictates what dress we may wear, how we may walk, lie down, eat, speak, — our rising up and sitting down are anathema or blessed as he decrees. He makes our houses places where congregate families beaten and scarred in the struggle with temptation. After long ages of obedience to him, we are told that life is a mystery and "there is no hope this side of the grave."

The East negates even the God-emanating. The West would legislate to the very heavens. Both systems are hints of the true. All religions have good in the germ. They swing around some central truth which is the deathless quality that has kept them from annihilation. The East and the West, they make the round world. All men are brothers, children of the same Father. "Hath not one God made you?" — "of one blood all the nations." Absolute truth is Freedom for every creature. Let us marry the still East to the forward moving West and make the rounded sphere of a perfect law for the sons and daughters of God. Let us speak aloud the secret, silent mysteries of Eastern symbology, and bring the gospel of satisfaction to every creature. Let us touch the still harp strings of Oriental mysticism with the trained winds of Occidental positivism, and ring forth a harmony to which the whole world can sing!

"Let there be light." As if the earth should do something — make some movement of her own to work her way from darkness into light. It is only "work out your own salvation" set to a secret, symbolic key. It is a lesson of life. Go ye into all the world teaching it.

Denials alone do not bring light; they do not bring full spiritual understanding, but only intimations of it. Freedom is not redemption. As when at night we disrobe, divest ourselves of bodily clothing, wash ourselves from contact with day, and go to our rest, so at night we may unburden our mind of the beliefs that have weighted it always, by denial, and breathe the clean air of blessed freedom from sordid cares. Denials are a soluble principle — a cleansing efficiency. They do their work as certainly as the life-principle within the seed bursts the choking pericarp, rifts the smothering soil and, defying the downward pressure of sun, gravitation and falling rains, will up into the blessed sunlight for fruitage and blossoming.

But the plant which has passed sordid blackness has to learn to appropriate — to use the light. The mind which has thrown off its false beliefs, must take on its true ones — its robes of righteousness.

A higher attenuation of error, a subtler temptation than has yet befallen, here awaits us. Only the holiest of the mystics have passed this point unscathed, and they have left no message so definite concerning their experience, that others who would follow them have passed the etherealized point under their guidance and come out and past knowing that upon foregoing material self the universe grows "I", and self spiritual a microcosm of the macrocosom — the "I", the perfect likeness of the "ALL" — *if the right word be spoken*: "And without him was not anything made that was made."

The power of the word to create, draw, bring knowledge, clothe upon, is that which they have not definitely taught us. Who could have gleaned the law from these words of the wonderful mystics of antiquity?

"It is not till we have pushed past the gateways of denial — the walls of sensation — and come out upon the open plains where we have cried, It is! It is! that we have drawn down excellence and proved ourselves the likeness of All Good."

The temptation to teach the loss of the individual self as a water drop in the ocean of Being, has been widely yielded to. But the great teacher whose words we have quoted, taught no such loss. He spoke of Abraham and Isaac and Jacob as still living. Moses and Elias lie made visible to his sordid companions. The eternality and ever responsibility of the "I", that wisest teacher among men taught. Who has not seen that life, to be practically worthwhile, must be individualized for working along some special line of endeavor — some line of recognized importance?

As in the morning we robe the body with fresh raiment to go forth to meet the day, so after the mind's rest in freedom from false beliefs, it should rise to clothe itself with robes of righteousness. Righteousness, according to the Kabala, is right thinking. Thoughts of error enswathed the mind. The word divested it of them. Thoughts of truth should clothe it. What words in the science of mental treatment have robing potency? Go ye into all the world preaching them, when once you have found them, for they are words of Eternal Life:

GOD IS LIFE, TRUTH, LOVE, SUBSTANCE, INTELLIGENCE, OMNIPRESENCE, OMNIPOTENCE, OMNISCENCE.

*God is Life*: I feel the waiting Silence stir. The vivific life-principle thrills and shivers through me.

*God is Truth*: What is it faces me with a sea of boundless Truth, lifting me from memory of the untrue material world, bearing me out upon the white billows of certainty that I know the Truth that will prevail?

*God is Love*: What is it satisfies me better than the love of family and kindred; folds me in its presence — making me forget pain, desolation, terror?

I shall not want, upon Thy arm relying;

Hunger, and cold and sorrow flee away,

And the dark valley where my hope was lying,

Doth shine like day when night hath gone away.

"Oh, blessed, broken heart," it whispers "See, I bind you up forever. Child of mind, I comfort you — 'as a mother comforteth.' Look up — 'Thy Maker is thy husband.' 'Thou shalt not be consumed with hunger in the land anymore.' Neither bear the reproach of the heathen anymore." Balm from old Gilead could not ease as these words ease the bruises of sorrow and misfortune. Love of God, I nevermore can doubt thee!

*God is Substance*: Something solidifies my being into conscious certainty of oneness with a Presence self-existent, changeless, eternal; a still nearness to which I may cling — upon which I may rest — my rock and my fortress unfailing. "They that trust in the Lord shall be as Mount Zion which cannot be moved, but abideth forever."

*God is Intelligence:* What flashes light through and around me, making me to know the presence of pure Intelligence of whose name-less wisdom I recognize myself the breath and utterance?

I recognize myself in recognizing what and where the being who created me surely is. To know myself and my mission through the eternities is absolutely necessary to my peace of mind. Many a great observer of life-purposes and life-desires has noted that the question put by every mind is, *Who am I, whither am I bound, and what is my mission?*

The highest wisdom of Greece was the precept over the Del-phic temple, *Know Thyself.* In the Vedanta philosophy of India, the oldest religious philosophy of the world, it is said, "There is nothing higher than the attainment of the knowledge of the Self. Despising, rejecting all else, a wise man should strive after the knowledge of his real self." The Self is called in the Vedanta, the "Silent Thinker, the inmost spring of thought. To discover the real self — to brush away the rubbish of false notions with respect to it, is the summit of all at-tainment.

A subtle error the child has made when entering into higher recognition of himself, has been to say, "I am God." Not so; one speaker is truer; "In my highest moment I enter in and know that I do not live — I am lived. I do not think — I am thought. I do not move — I am moved." Another said, "The words that I speak unto you it is not I that speak, but the Father that dwelleth in me, He doeth the works." Still another said, "In Him we live, and move, and have our being." "We are not sufficient to think anything as of ourselves."

Then this must be a great truth that swells for utterance con-cerning myself, when I have spoken the words naming the Being of Deity; *I am thine idea O God, and in thee I live and move and have my being.* The words are spoken — I have cast away anxious care con-cerning myself. He *careth* for me. Thoughts spring fresh and majestic — "O God, I am thinking thy thoughts after Thee!"

*I am Spirit. Mind. Like Thee, and reflect Wisdom, Strength, Holi-ness.* How certainly He keepeth me from unwise speaking and unnec-essary doing. What trust springs up in the excellence of the judgment that moves upon the demands of the hour so strangely through myself!

*God works through me to will and to do that which ought to be done by me:* What is this strong conviction of a potency flowing through me, and beyond me, following my thoughts to make them efficient to touch with healing, love, and joy, whatever they reach, returning again to myself making me strong to know and to do?

*I am governed by the law of God and cannot sin, cannot suffer for sin, nor fear sin, sickness, or death.*

I feel myself one with the stem Law-Giver, as the Law Principle moves and establishes every good work it wills to do through me, to turn and overturn old thoughts and ways till it whose right it is to reign, stands fixed, immovable, stern law against my sinning — against all sin — all fear of sin — making me a strong tower against the surging machinations of evil in whatever form, fastening me securely to the "Rock that is higher than I" — out of the reach of death and the grave.

The spiritual faculty awakens. Secrets kept from the foundation of the world become ours — "not lawful to utter!" The white sun-fire of immortal Truth shines over, warming and lifting us above the cold black belief of death and dying into the hot glory of living service for the world. These are affirmations of universal and omnipresent Good. They are words pungent and sweet and reviving like the wines of the sunny islands, lifting men off beds of pain and languishing, into health that makes life forever and forever worth the living.

To the homesick wanderer, rest and peace. To the parched earth-traveler, living waters. To the tired mother, they are words of gladness wafting across her white face airs from the hill-tops of the land toward which her weary feet hasten — glad foretaste of the time when "there shall be no more pain, neither sorrow nor crying, for the former things have passed away." And to all who say them knowing why they are true, sweet assurances of favor with Omnipotence and signs of growth in grace and goodness.

As the plant draws from the sun carbon and mineral salts, the warm constituents of inorganic growth, and from the airs and rains and sands the organic ingredients for bloom and fruitage, so thou, sweet child of light, mayest from all things now call new knowledge down. Thou shalt be in league with the silent springs of all things. They shall have voices to teach thee. The trees that lean and whisper against the far horizon shall tell thee words true and deathless. Suns in the distant zenith throw beams of love and wisdom down. Winds blowing hot from Spiced Araby and cold from the white northlands, sing of home and love and youth. "Thou shalt be in league with the stones of the field, and the beasts of the field shall be at peace with thee."

"Prove thyself' — "Prove Me Now."

# LESSON FOUR

## Science is Systematized Knowledge

Mental Science must be a description and explanation of mental processes and experiences. Christian Science must be a description and explanation of Truth.

Science is systematized knowledge.

Systematized knowledge of Truth is but another name for Christian Science, since Christ means Truth, and careful and descriptive explanation of Christian principles and laws is Christian Science.

In all Science, the steps are sequential. That is, one step follows another reasonably. In revolutionizing the mind's beliefs by a new set of arguments, the turns of change follow each other with unvarying order. In changing the shadow view on a screen from the wrong to the right side up, the view follows the turn in the camera, whether it be made rapidly or slowly. If the mind be open and receptive, the change will be instantaneous, to be sure, but still it must go from wrong to right by regular gradations.

Full perception of Truth is like a blaze of light over dense darkness. But perception of Truth that saves is a spiritual awakening which has not come while the mind still opposes any objections or is obliged to question the way. Hence, the mental change from ignorance to knowledge is slow to us all, and we are quite able to describe and explain the phenomena of passage from darkness to light. These are identical, each with the other, the world over, the only difference being the difference of time different minds take to apprehend the same Truth or to become spiritually awake.

Of course, you understand, the whole scheme of the science is to spiritualize the mind, or to evolve it into the light of understanding. The process and intent are not new. The whole aim of students of real life through the ages, has been to teach the race its privileges. They have spoken for the most part incoherently, because they have also spoken of other laws besides the spiritual, and have not explicitly defined the distinction. But in moments of highest realization of Truth as related to Life, they have all said the same things.

Taking the same premise how could they other than conclude the same way? Science is science, and whether it is a problem in life or mathematics, exact calculation from a given premise must of necessity result the same, no matter who calculates, or when the calculation.

The astronomers of Gizeh, prophesying when a Draconis would cease to be North Star, and a Polaris reign in its stead, must of necessity have struck the exact date that the British astronomer of to-day computes as having been the time of the change. Taking the unit one for their starting point, mathematics drove them both to one and the same conclusion.

Taking the spiritual origin of all things, the students of life must teach one and the same law of life. If one states this law, and then disputes it, we may not know whether to believe him or not, but it would be worthwhile to examine the argument, which has struck universally in the problem of life the same statements, with as unvarying similarity as mathematicians have shown in scientific computation.

Many of these students of life have veered from this basis, and given us veering conclusions. As, after stating the spiritual and death-less origin of the race, and its spiritual and deathless quality, "He who thinks that he can slay a Life, or he who thinks Life can be slain, These both do err, for life is God, and God cannot be slain." These students talked of death and the ways of death as if death were as real as life. Thus they have spoken incoherently and have puzzled the simple children who did not notice that their teachers took certain things for granted by one line of reasoning, and utterly repudiated them by another. But, forgetting their suppositions and terrors, in exalted moments of certainty, they have all vehemently declared the same things:

All evil is so much negation — non-entity.

"He beholdeth all there is,"

and "He beholdeth not iniquity."

There is no iniquity with the Lord God, and no respect of persons.

Sometimes this law of the unreality of what seems, or is perceived by sensation, was told of old by myth or allegory; and whoever is bold and unprejudiced enough to take the meaning, has the key to the knowledge of all things. One whose inner vision is opened like Swedenborg's, often sees great truths in pictures or symbols, which, when they are told or described, are called myths.

A myth is a fabulous or imaginary tale told to illustrate some great truth. There is an ancient myth told by a seer of symbolic visions, who saw the state of all mankind as chained in a rock cave with their faces to the plane of its sides, so that they never saw real objects, but only the shadows of them; and from this imprisonment they could never be free till by some violent wrenching of their own effort they should break the chains that bound them, and turn to behold real objects and each other aright.

"Who would be free, themselves must strike the blow."

Now, the explanation of the myth is that mankind has been looking at shadow, and not substance., because man has taken the appearance for the reality. The senses give appearances only. The appearance must be rectified by some higher faculty than physical sight. The senses tell that the sun arises and sets, but science explains that sunrise and sunset are appearances only.

A distinguished writer upon science notes that the effect of the study of natural science is to breed a wholesome skepticism in the mind regarding the evidence of the senses. The sky seems to be a solid vault, but science proves it penetrable ether. Stars look like points of light, but science discovers them to be suns and worlds. When the blinds are drawn aside, the sunlight pouring into a dark room makes us suppose its light was entirely from without, but science explains that it is light from within springing to meet the light without.

That which is true of the wide external universe, is also true of the child of the universe. Appearances tell that he is imperfect and miserable, the creation of a Being capable of making imperfect creatures; but Science, which deals with principles, reasons him out as the idea of Eternal Mind, the creation of a Being incapable of making anything unlike himself. Science calling reason into action respecting these things, finds that man, as he seems, with all the phenomena that surround him, is the phantasmagoric and unreal shadow of the unseen divine idea, which reasoning or right thinking reveals, placing the reasoner one with the Mind that thinks him. Kepler, when he had discovered the law of planetary motion and distance, catching the idea of unvarying law, cried out, "O God, I think thy thoughts after Thee!"

I speak of the marvelous effect of right thinking or silent wording. The science of mind lays great stress upon the force and practical effect of right words. "A right word, how good it is." "Who can measure the force of a right word?" "He sent forth his word and healed them." Five hundred years after him another declared that "All that we are and all that we see is built by our thought." One came speaking as having authority to declare from the foundation of absolute knowledge, "According to thy faith be it unto thee."

The words of Science are first a revelation; second, the opening of prison doors. With the denials we catch breaths from the fair hills of freedom. With the affirmations courage and assurance from the mountains round about Jerusalem. We come nearer to knowing divine realities. We see that it is the out-picturing of erroneous reasoning with no foundation in Truth that claims to be pain, sickness, imperfection. We think of the years of experience with bitterness, failure, on-coming age, liability to loss of loved ones, inability to cope with the world, as dreams — "as a dream when one awaketh." *Now we know.*

If thoughts make us what we seem, and thoughts are controllable, then to control thoughts aright is to show forth rightly. "The primitive mind", says a noted college president, "takes appearance for reality." The appearances are that external conditions control thoughts, not that thoughts control conditions. Whoever accepts the appearance for the reality in this particular, proves himself unlearned and untaught in the laws of mind.

The law of the effect of silent thought, known, proves thoughts to be first. One is sick or diseased, or in pain and fever; we think a healing thought, and its symbol is at hand, as soothing balm, or healing arnics, or cooling nitre. We see only the symbols and apply them, thinking they have in themselves intrinsic excellence. But it is, only mind, catching the idea of the soothing and healing they stand for. If we would put the symbol to one side and acknowledge the idea — keep the saying — the healing thought — we would bring quicker healing. It is a medicine that we need never be without. "I will never leave thee nor forsake thee." "Acknowledge me."

Certain kinds of thoughts bring sickness (in the realm of mortal mind). If we are trained in the laws of thought we refuse to harbor them. Then we are never sick. If we think only thoughts of health and strength, we shall be health and strength centers, from which will constantly go forth healing and strengthening thoughts. "Let your light shine."

This science is young with us. Our thoughts of healing go out tremblingly to meet the dark opposition of mortal appearances. We are not grounded sufficiently into belief in the power of Truth when we speak it, to hold steadfastly certain that the silent word we bring, being the righteous word, will prevail. Hence there is much failure of proof, on the part of the young scientists, that they are in the right. That is, they fail in healing the sick sometimes — apparently.

All failure is sign of fear, and fear is sign of doubt in the power of Truth. And doubt has its root in lack of understanding of the principle upon which healing arguments are based, or from which they spring forth. It is not till the mind has risen beyond the obedient thinking of right thoughts according to rule, or under direction, into understanding of Principle, that it cannot be shaken or fail to prove the power of Truth.

It is the province of science to train mind into such understanding as not to fail. They that understand are the trusting, of whom it is written, "Like Mount Zion, which cannot be moved, but abideth forever." The boy at the board not understanding the principle he is dealing with, is open to a rule not right; but when he understands, the wrong rule is absurdity and he keeps steadfastly on to right results.

Those upon whom understanding has not flashed are shaky, sometimes performing miracles of cure, but feeling no assurance of right so strong but opposing arguments, or fears of bodily pain, or adversity, make them half-hearted, and drive them to medication and worldly schemes again.

We must learn to stand steadfastly against the surges of fear, the waves of opposing thoughts. There must be a firm mind to battle the ebbing and flowing currents of scorn and favor, "Let there be a firmament in the midst of the waters." Let there be a definite appearing — a certainty as to where you stand and what you believe.

Nothing can be more delightful than the strength of affirmation when it is first learned. We think we have found the key to the solution of the great problem of life. "Now all things are to be ours through the power of the word." We can hardly contain our joy at the new-found treasure. But, "Let there be a firmament" means something. Let there be a firm *mans*, a firm or definite certainty of mind.

If the denials and affirmations with their spiritualizing results were the end of our effort, the way would be easy. For the experiences that come are independent of effort. But the world of sense meets us when we are most assured — its hard practicalities strike us. The talk and the conduct, the learning and the laws of the land are all against us. Where is the kingdom of heaven or state of harmony that has been preached to us, into which it is promised we shall enter? According to the evidence of the senses, *nowhere!*

Where is the accomplishing power named by us? Nothing of our saying has proved itself true. Our word has no more changing power than formerly. "I do not believe this science," we cry in grief or anger of disappointment. But the trial of your faith worketh patience and patience godliness, and godliness the peaceable fruits of righteousness — the fruits of right thinking. When the plant is just set free into the spring airs, it does not find its first faculty capable of bringing forth. The airs are keen, the way toward fruitage long. Having been set free from darkness, it is met by the cold.

The mathematician, having announced his principle and begun the calculation with given propositions, finds some point where the problem looks formidable. He must have faith in his rules and the necessity for the solution of the problem to keep on with the majestic and as yet unsolved question.

We must have faith in our rules, and the necessity for the solution of the life problem.

We have said, "God works through me to will and to do that which ought to be done by me." We have virtually surrendered our will to the Divine Will. But the conscious mind finds it quite another matter to reconcile the statement to appearances.

The conflict between scientific statement and phenomenal or material environment breeds doubt. Doubt in the phenomenal? No, doubt in the science. In every department of science the conflict between scientific statement and phenomenal environment is apparent disaster to science. "Choose ye this day whom ye will serve" — Truth that *is*, or error that *seems*.

Doubt grows unsown, bred by the nature of things. Not doubt of the false (that seems the most real thing in the universe), but doubt of the true, which must be proved true before it can satisfy the mind with certainty. Shall we keep on with the new, or go back to the old? "Choose ye!"

Faith is the most intense form of mental action. Faith by careful statement is born through sore travail. We must give birth to it by a volitional effort of the will.

*I will believe in the statements of Science. They are true.*

The prophets and bards and seers of old taught that these things are true. Jesus of Nazareth set his seal and sign-manual upon them. I do believe that the Good, the Best, is the true; the evil is false and has no space or place in a universe created by the Good, occupied by the Good, and tolerating only good!

*Though I see not, yet will I believe!*

"Blessed are they that have not seen, and yet have believed," Choose — choose well — choose ye God and all nature waits your lonely choice. If you choose feebly, your work will be feeble. "According to thy faith be it unto thee."

Here eyes do regard you in eternity's stillness,

Choose well, your choice is brief, and yet endless.

Laws and principles are not for times of quiet contemplation, and hours of ease; they are for the battle ground of daily experience, when temptations beset and failures try their quality. "If thou faint in the day of adversity thy strength is small."

In the gospels, men are blamed for not having faith. This would be hard and unkind if there were not some proper ground for faith. The proper ground for faith to rest upon is a foundation in reason why certain things are true. We must have a "reason for the hope that is in us."

We notice that they are blessed who not having seen yet have believed; but faith is not demanded of us in blindness. Luther, Anselm, and many wise teachers wrested the Scriptures to read that we must believe before we can know; but the Scriptures only say "Blessed are they that have not seen, and yet have believed." They do not demand faith without a reason for faith.

The proper ground for faith in every department of science is knowledge of the law of relations — that is, by knowing that certain things are true, we are obliged to conclude that certain other things are true. Axioms in mathematics are conclusions based upon unchangeable relations. "The whole is equal to the sum of all its parts." Thus, the parts being given, we are obliged to believe that their sum is the whole. Faith is conviction based upon knowledge. Galileo knew that the earth rotated on its axis west to east, and was obliged to believe that the sun did not rise and set.

The reason for faith in health and strength and perfect living, is the law of *promissum*, whereby things sent beforehand are promises of things to be — foretastes of things shortly to come to pass. What is it that is sent beforehand to the children of the Science? An axiom is immutable and unvarying law; "Whatsoever things ye desire, when ye pray, believe that you receive, and ye shall receive."

Why should you believe that you receive? Because health and strength and perfect living are the desires of the heart. Desires are things sent before, signals thrown out, signs by the way of things that we have a right to. "Wait patiently on the Lord, and he shall give thee the desires of thine heart." Not the things you do not want, but the things that you really want. Not some things, but *whatsoever things*. Not sometimes receive, but always receive, provided you believe that you receive.

Why should the health you have affirmed, the peace and freedom you have declared, be believed in as already received? Because they are good. And all things good are already created, waiting in the invisible silence for your word to speak of them till they come manifestly present. I do not make the law, but only read out of the law that good things shall wait upon true prayer, warmed and vivified by faith. "Faith is the substance of things hoped for, the evidence of things not seen." What we believe, that will come to pass "What the spirit promises, nature will perform."

But outward things and conditions are now directly opposite to our scientific statement. "We cannot believe," we say, "against sense evidence." "The trial of your faith."

I will believe. "Though he slay me, yet will I trust Him!" Because God is! Because God makes, I believe in the good as the only reality. I do believe in the good as the true and this which is evil I will not believe in.

Every mind must come to the ground bed of its own quality to spring forth its thoughts from its own faith.

And mind is not worth much till it is tried in the furnace of opposition, seeming failure and desolation. But, knowing the law, of ever present good through opposition, disappointment, poverty, hardship, ignominy, death, desertion, to stand and wait the fulfillment of law — the coming to pass — this is faith.

In the eager quest for health we have leaned upon many things to help and aid us to it. But they have all failed us because they were not substantial. They were substanceless. They were temporal fleeting signs of a deathless excellence, which we might have laid hold upon to lead us into health that would not fail, and strength that would never leave us.

The sick have leaned upon herbs and compounded drugs of many a sort. Certain physical constitutions would recuperate sometimes at the idea of renewal which these things suggested, but for the most part they failed, and there has been weary turning from them toward other things.

Tenderer than the ointments of the good Samaritan is the gentle word that touches the bruised hope and the broken heart — "Thy words were found, and I did eat them, and thy word was unto me the joy and rejoicing of mine heart." The words that rejoice and make glad the heart, the words that lift the fainting hopes, they are the words that heal from sickness — they are "health to all flesh."

People sometimes lean upon the aid and skill of some departed friend, or one who has once lived on this earth in the physical body, who can now work his will through them to accomplish healing. They surrender their own consciousness, for the time being, to another's. That other does through them, as mediums of its will, the works they ask.

One point to be noticed in the Science of Being, is the eternal responsibility of the consciousness.

To submit to the will and consciousness of a less than God, for any purpose whatsoever, is to manifest deterioration. The limp and inferior quality of mentality which we see those exhibit who surrender their will and mind to another will and mind less than God, is the mark of disobedience. "Thou shalt not bow down," (yield) "Nor serve" — "obey, but one, and He thy God."

All things not The Good fail us; so they who lean -upon, or trust anything but *It*, find that which they lean upon forsaking them in due season. The one who has worked his will through the willing medium finds himself pushed on to fulfill his Father's commands, and leaves his servant helpless and hopeless. "Put not your trust in princes." But Omnipotence working through you "will never leave you, nor forsake you"

Some have trusted to animal magnetism, a subtle fluid proceeding from all fleshly organisms, which, they believe, regulates by stimulating or retarding physical functions and activities. But the regulating power of animal magnetism soon reaches its height, breaks and dies away into powerlessness. Only the sweet influence of the Spirit lives on forever, increasing in efficiency, "shining more and more unto the perfect day."

People of a certain class of mind have been tempted to heal by the power of the human will. They are those who have the power to concentrate all their forces for a single purpose. Mesmer was the most successful practitioner in this line we have any record of. It is sometimes called Mesmerism after him. A weak and sick person is a good subject for the exercise of the ability. The poor helpless finds his own will whiffed aside like a candle-flame in the wind, and while the impetus of the stronger will is upon him he is obediently well. But when time or absence breaks the spell, "the last state of that man is worse than the first."

God is the only Will that abides,

Though the human will doth falter;

The strong Power that lives through time,

The high Thought that cannot alter.

# LESSON FIVE

## Look to God

It will be seen by the lessons thus far, that according to the principles of Spiritual Science, it is a waste of time, and the evidence of an untaught mind, to lean for health upon any material aid.

All systems that teach us to look to liquids, solids, gases, for bodily health, are carnal, for they do not bring the health that is expected; they only seem to for a little while, then suddenly fail. They teach the mind to repose upon unrealities, to hope reality or good to itself from shadows.

Yet it is right to lean upon something, to hope for health and satisfaction from something outside of ourselves.

Many ethical teachers have taught that we can hope for no satisfaction from outside sources. But they have overlooked the law of fulfillment of instincts. The impulse to fly is a sign there is air to fly in; the impulse to walk, is a sign there is ground to walk on; the impulse to swim, is a sign there is water to swim in. The impulse or instinct to lean upon something to make us well, is a sign that there is something that will make us well. The impulse or instinct to lean upon something to make us happy is a sign that there is something that will make us happy.

Yet nothing that we have leaned upon, has made us well or happy. So as the sign never fails to be true, it shows we have not leaned upon the right things. Why? Because, being spirit, we have leaned upon matter for health; being mind, we have looked to physical things for satisfaction. We have not paid any attention to the imperative command, heard over all the rush and noise of our dealings with our fellow-beings — "Look unto me, and be ye saved all the ends of the earth."

Looking to God means seeing and knowing that the good is, and where it is. When we know that it is here all about us, waiting for us to acknowledge it, then we are looking to it. Then exactly the blessing we want comes to us. But we must acknowledge it; that is, we must speak it

Many people have a good theory about this, telling how surely their faith is very great, and the thrills of spiritual influx make them sure of great power. But they cannot heal themselves; their troubles in life are fearful. They talk in one breath of how great their faith in this principle is, and in the next breath of how much they suffer.

Truth is a silent principle. It never shows till it is spoken. "Acknowledge *me* in all thy ways."

Truth is Peace itself. They who suffer are not in peace; then they have not spoken Truth. We desire peace. The desire is a promise (*promissum*), that we may have peace by saying that we have it already.

Some object that it seems as if they were telling a lie, by saying they are not in pain or trouble, when they are in agony and groaning.

Jesus of Nazareth did exactly that. When he was on the cross, not yet dead in the flesh, according to belief, He said "It is finished." He did not prove that his necessity for going through torture was past until he *said* it was past or finished.

"The word was God — and without him was not anything made that was made." That is, nothing is proved until the word about it was spoken. Nothing shows up, or out, or forth, till we speak the word. with authority, that it is so.

If you are desolate or lonely, or desire reconciliation with loved ones, the desire is a promise that there is love and companionship awaiting you. Love is a still Principle, invisible; speak it into outward showing. In this still, invisible Presence is everything you desire; say understandingly that it is already received by you. The time of its coming will be slow or quick according to your understanding; never mind the time of your answer.

Stick to the word of Truth; talk about it as already here, although no one may see it. "You shall receive." It is the law of the externalizing power of the word. You may speak it silently or audibly. If you speak it audibly, people may think you are mad or foolish. It is better to speak these things in the silence, to avoid controversy. Controversy is the appearance of evil. "Avoid the appearance of evil" They that know the law can afford to wait on the Lord, or law.

Do not let anybody or anything beat you down, or argue you off your basis, whether it is attempted by people in the body of flesh, or in the belief of an astral body, out of the flesh. Those out of the flesh are no wiser than those in the flesh, if they say that the thing you desire cannot be made to come to you.

Some make the mistake of thinking that they must choose only such blessings as may be best for them. But the desire in all instances is a hint of the thing we ought to have. To say that the will of God is to be done, and to submit to it with certainty that it is the good, will in every instance end in the blessing coming about according to our desires.

To fear that we shall be answered in some other way is to get the answer some other way. "The thing I feared is come upon me." Fear shows externally as things we do not desire. All troublous circumstances, all physical imperfections, are out-picturing of false thoughts — thoughts naming a law other than the perfectly desirable.

Swedenborg saw the symbolisms that all things make; that is, he saw that all things are symbols of ideas or thoughts. If he had seen that only the good is symbolized, and seen that to name the good as all, would prove it so, his system of correspondence by symbolisms would have saved the world from its misconception of Bible translations.

"And without Him was not anything made that was made." God is too pure to behold iniquity. "There is no iniquity with the Lord God, and no respect of persons." Make both the desire and the heart that desires, to be in their natures and essence divine, because divinely created. To declare them evil, either the desire of the heart or the heart that desires, is to speak falsely of divine things.

If one says that this argument makes the desire for tobacco, strong drink, and other vicious tastes, righteous desires — why, no.

They do not exist. No desire for the undesirable has existence. The error is in supposing that it is strong drink, as such, that people want. It is the craving thirst for or after righteousness, given. It is the restless desire for satisfaction seeking a false channel. To rouse and say to such an appetite, "It is not strong drink that is wanted; it is strong thoughts; it is thoughts that shall satisfy as thirst is quenched," is to find the old appetite fall away, and a nameless peace stealing over.

All desire still remains, sign of a right which the law recognizes. "Blessed are they that hunger and thirst after righteousness, for they shall be filled." "They shall hunger no more, neither thirst anymore," who enter the kingdom of knowing that all is Mind and Mind's ideas — not flesh, and the tastes of flesh at all.

In the desire for health, it seems that we are to put no trust in any material aid, prop or comfort. But we are shown a better way, shown better things to lean upon.

When Jesus of Nazareth had carefully instructed his disciples to put no trust in earthly things, he told them to cast all care upon God. Moth and rust corrupt and decay earthly things, making them unreliable. He showed them that the law being that God always careth for those who trust, they need not worry about right provisions.

Then they began to mourn about his word, prophesying his leaving them. They were hanging with child-like trust upon his miraculous power to provide all things for them. He had provided just what they needed, always out of nothing at all, apparently, or from the most uncompromising conditions. So they leaned on him.

When they pressed their mourning thought upon him, he said — "I will not leave you comfortless. He (The Father) shall give you another Comforter, that he may abide with you forever, even the Spirit of Truth." "And the Comforter is come, whom I will send unto you from the Father, even the Spirit of Truth, he will guide you into all Truth."

Many are mourning at the statements of Divine Science. It seems as if the Jesus of Theology were taken away, when we say it is only the word of Truth spoken that saves us from evil. It seems as if we have nothing to cling to. But we have the same Comforter he told about. The word that we speak brings Love itself to our aid, and this is proved by our satisfaction with the conditions that begin to surround us. We begin to be loved by every one, and to love every one. We do not have to try to make people love us; they cannot help it. We do not have to try love people; we cannot help it.

The Spirit of Truth is the Word of Truth. To cling to this word will lead us into all Truth, where we cannot get mixed up with all sorts of strange claims and doctrines that are not truth at all. This word is what we are commanded to preach and teach, and it is promised that it will be the salvation of all who hear it. You need not try to get saved; the Truth will save you. Whoever will give you the full statement of Truth, has set your mind into the way of salvation from its errors.

People preach a bit of Truth and mix it with a lot of error, and then they wonder why they do not convert people to their way of thinking. They teach us that some of us are to be lost, that some of us cannot learn spiritual things, that even little children are to be burned for their sins, that if we do not believe just what they teach, we shall have the same fate.

The perfect word is quick and powerful to the saving efficiency. Peter proved this, when with one Pentecostal sermon he added to his church, 3,000 converts.

Men willingly turn from error when the real Truth is spoken. Truth spoken is a working principle that will never leave them if someone speaks it to them.

No matter who speaks Truth, no matter what religion you find it in, no matter how clumsily Truth is told, when it is told, that is the whole Truth, people must be saved. They must be made whole. They will be comforted. As one whom his mother comforteth, so will they be comforted. "Thy God hath called thee as a woman forsaken and grieved." "The father of the fatherless." But we cannot get this until we do acknowledge or speak Truth, nor get quick help until we trust, or understand it to be Truth.

Everything teaches us to trust, because everything is a sign of the law of unvarying fitness. "The invisible things of God," Paul says, "are clearly seen by the things that are made." He means that the good things invisible are made manifest by outward signs.

The Scriptures tell us how we go from ignorance, which is darkness, to understanding, which is light. We go by steps. We may take them rapidly or slowly.

"Let the waters be gathered together unto one place, and let the dry land appear."

As the establishing of a firmament is equivalent to the conscious choice by us, to hold to truth itself, when all things seem to oppose, so the waters have their significance in telling that story which is a picture of mental history. "Waters" signify the conscious mind that changes, that varies, and gives us animate character. And the "dry land" represents the settled convictions, the fixed ideas that make our character fixed, and is called in Christian Science the unconscious mind. The settled convictions of the mind externalize themselves as the body of fleshy organs, while the active conscious thoughts seem always to express themselves by the blood. "The blood is the life thereof," and "the word is the life thereof," or the blood shows constantly your active thoughts as your words (silent or audible) speak or show them. Two ways of telling the same story.

That choking sarcasm that your conscious thought holds, whether speaking through your lips or silently felt, changes second by second, the constitution and quality of your blood. And the blood changes the character and tone of the organic and functional departments of the body. That scorn and criticism you hold against another in your conscious mind is affecting the harmonious mixture of warm red blood globules, rapidly transforming them to watery humors and acid secretions — photographing by a law of mental photography upon a sensitive plate called physical body, every thought that you harbor.

Swedenborg says that changing conscious thoughts change the lungs, heart, stomach and liver with lightning-like rapidity, as the pictures on the screen change with the movements of the slide in the magic lantern.

A warm sympathetic thought for a friend or foe suddenly begins to transform the watery, acid humors of the blood to red globules rich with albumen and iron, or the sweetness and strength of better character.

If you say to me that some good, generous people are sick and bloodless, you must be told that it is wrong, and damaging to health, to think evil or ill of ourselves as of others, and they think themselves great sinners. To hold in your mind that you are or have been a great sinner is to carry a burden that will show and hold as a withering body. To live in the realization of other people's belief about us, that we are or have been great sinners, is to show the belief forth as weakness or disease. Make no error with your thoughts. Compel them to think only right and good things at all times.

The word spoken silently or audibly, by us, is the conscious thought, or conscious mind, for which we are constantly responsible, and which, after being harbored by us is perpetually settling back into unconsciousness, and writing itself as the physical organs or conscious mind.

In the book, S & H,[2] you will find these divisions of the mind that externalizes as body, as denominated conscious and unconscious mortal mind, mortal mind, meaning the error mind or counterfeit mind, in its varied operations of thinking or supposing that things going on in the material world are real and true and actual transactions, instead of only mirage images of some ideas that are moving in the Eternal Mind.

The mortal conscious mind (that supposes its body which it forms by thinking thoughts is the real body, and itself the real self) is the puzzle word of the metaphysicians, the rock of stumbling.

They say to each other, "If the mortal mind makes mistakes and there is but one mind and that is God, do you not see you make out by this argument that the mind that is God, which is the only mind, makes mistakes?" No, says the metaphysician. It is hard to define and explain a negation. Still if one has understanding, another may have the same.

In the universe, there is the ALL and the nothing. This is axiomatic truth. Now if the ALL is eternal, immortal mind, the nothing must be temporal, mortal, no-mind, pure nothing, no mind at all.

---

[2] *Science and Health with Key to the Scriptures* by Mary Baker Eddy, founder of the Church of Christ, Scientist, which became known as the Christian Science Church.

The ALL Mind is Immortal Mind. The no-mind is mortal. Among the ancients it was declared that the moving law of the visible universe is Adonia — copy of real — shadow of substance — the law that moves the procession of things we see with the eyes of flesh. But the real Principle of all the vivific principle, is Akasa or Deity, the unnameable. From it emanates the deathless real soul of man.

He who knows the real, loses sight of the unreal sense-world, or material, and turns materiality into nothingness. Then he sees realities, and all things are transformed. Where the material seemed to be with no good in it for him, all grows spiritual and gives him real good.

The moving law of deception claims to be intelligence moving. Its name, with all its claims, is Adonia or Adam, the highest law of earthly things, animal man, psychic soul. The symbolism or shadow is not wickedness, though it may believe itself wicked and seem to show it. It is simple shadow, inverted mirage image of something real and true. To say that it has dominion over us, either as to power to bring disease or pain, or to determine against or for according to its own will, is to give dominion and power to non-intelligence.

Error, or mistake, which is evil, is that which might be, if good were not all; a supposition of what would be if Truth were not omnipresent. Error is simply nothing, named where substance occupies all place, a supposition where truth fills all space, as a supposition that 9 and 1 are 12, where 10 is always true. In mathematics you suppose $x$ to be the value of the grain, but the true value of the grain is not $x$; its true value is a mathematical certitude, with which all the universe is filled; that is, it is true everywhere, lying in silence as Truth everywhere true, *waiting to be spoken.*

What we call mortal mind, is just like that $x$, which has no value whatever. It is nothing but a claim to be something, which is erased, or removed from sight, instantly, when the Truth, which is here all the time — not spoken — is announced.

The mind that is God, is the Truth that is everywhere true. Spoken as Truth out of its tabernacles of silence, it becomes MANIFESTLY true, where it was true all the time but not spoken.

The *not spoken,* or not proved, is the negation which to be pure negation, must say or imply, that that is true which is not true. In other words, negation, nonentity, is called error, which is the Adam or a-dam (meaning error). It claims to be the true child of God, but belief in this claim is death. But in Christ, which is Truth spoken, or the word made flesh or made manifest, proved, expressed, if we believe, or have faith in, or trust utterly, we shall all be made alive.

It is written that in Adam all die, but in Christ all are made alive. That is but another way of expressing this thought. If we believe in the law of unreality, or dust, we are led to the death, but if we deny them and declare only Christ Truth about all things, we truly LIVE. Not until the fleshly or earthly man knows that he is nothing, and no names himself and declares for what is true, will he prove the Truth. Not until he reaches the positive statement against all negation., will he begin to prove it.

We must eat the flesh and drink the blood of Christ, or we must let the same mind be in us that Jesus of Nazareth had. We must let his words abide in us, by positive insistence, till in both conscious and unconscious mind we are at one with Truth, and have lost all consciousness of the law of matter. This sounds to some like a hard doctrine, to some easy.

When He said to His disciples, "The flesh profiteth nothing," many of them went back and walked no more with him. They were putting their dependence upon material, physical good, and could not bear to say it profited nothing, or could not bring them any good.

How many are like that now, they cling to their families with the desperate clutch of human love, and expect them to live, and be well, and to comfort them. To cling to physical human beings expecting much profit from them, and much good, is to cling to unreality, and this is proved by the fact that our clinging destroys them.

The spirit will return us all good. The flesh will begin to decay, and die if we fasten our minds upon it. Look at the miserable sickly bodies of the people who are idolized. They are eaten up by those who expect so much help and comfort from them. See children's inactive functions and discordant fretfulness. Foolish fondness, foolish eagerness to keep their bodies with us, is spoiling them. But to think of the deathlessness of the spirit, to think of their real nature, and let it work out as it will, is to let them into free air. They cannot be ill or die when we think of them *as they really are*, for it is meant that they should be with us always.

He who believes in evil, puts his dependence upon nothing, for what we believe in, we are putting dependence upon, and expecting something from. We get results according to the nature of that we look to. We look to error or mistakes for results, and are rewarded with the coldness of fear, and finally the belief in the ultimate power of evil, which is death.

The truth is always with us, for it is omnipresent. It speaks in the silence to the silent mind of us all. It is the Christ with us always, slain from the foundation of the world of negation, by the noisy, cruel, mortal error or mortal intellect, which will not listen.

Hush all the rush and noise of your consciousness, and listen to the silent law, that speaks within you. Wait, it is the true self, the God created, speaking in every man and woman and child.

Phythagoras called that silent self-law the salt of man in all ages, and the everlasting fountain of virtue. Plutarch called it the unerring guide. Socrates called it the good demon, not demon as the rendering is, but *daimon*, which means, Divine Self. John called it "the light that lighteth every man that cometh into, the world." Emerson said, stop all conscious thoughts, and wait for that silent schoolmaster to speak to you, and you will be told exactly what to do to make the greatest success in life, and each day's work will be mapped out plainly before you. Do this in the hush of the early morning.

It is the unerring counselor, the Actual of our being. The God-Self or goodself of us, eternally wise, immortal, vested with dominion over all things in earth, air and sea. When we listen to it, we drop this old man with his deeds, as Paul says, and bring immortality to light, or make it manifest here in a self that is not afraid of death, or anything that leads to, or threatens death.

It will teach us how to heal from sickness, how to conduct our business affairs, how to preach, teach, live exactly the right way, to make the most of ourselves here and now. It is the light of our being shining right here, while we are looking at the nothing, the nonspoken, the claim, or dark shadow, or rather while the not-spoken or nothing side claims a presence, name and way of working.

Now when the Truth is spoken to the error it is not always made immediately manifest. The intellectual or sense side claims power, and claims responsibility, and therefore must consent by its own word to be taught at the feet of the science, or work, or word of the Divine Presence. When we first hear or accept the Truth, it is by intellectual assent or with the conscious mind. We repeat the words that carry with them dematerializing effectiveness.

Soon the temptations to doubt the Truth, in one way or another face us. Even if we thought we believed them, with a knowledge of why they must be true according to a reckoning by intellect, or by logical conclusion, still some one or other point of evil looks real to us. Either matter with its apparent lies seems to us a thing not to be got rid of, or sin seems horribly present with us, or sorrow is our real enemy.

People tell about their spiritual understanding, and the next moment they rehearse the particulars of somebody's sickness, or somebody's wrong-doing or their troubles. If they understood the law, they could not thus tell over what is not true, they would know that it helps keep Truth from showing to talk about untruth. We have heard the law, by the hearing of the ear of intellect, or consciousness, but it has not become fixed oneness with ourselves.

Some people who have been very religious, but who have done some wrong things, so that their conscience burdens them, so that they feel guilty all the time, cannot speak of themselves as not under the law of sin. They will not be set free from sin till they do speak of themselves as already free. They can say "I am spiritual, not material." This is easy to them because it is a part of the teachings of the old philosophy that all is mind or spirit. But they cannot yet say there is no evil.

Others have studied about rocks and stars, bones and flesh and they can say "There is no evil" readily enough, but they are still hoping to get a great deal of pleasure out of physical things, and cannot deny them.

Some have lost some loved one by death and cannot say understandingly, "There is no death." It seems the most real of all to them. But in a universe where the ALL IS GOOD, THE ALL IS LIFE, death cannot be true. The Good does not chill, and benumb, and terrify its children. It gives them what they desire, and love and pray for.

The mortal belief of or in sin or evil, is all the evil there is. That which believes in evil is no mind. Mortality cannot conceive either of nothing or something. Mortal mind claims to be thinking, and claims to be something. It thinks nothing, and is nothing.

If you stand on a bridge over a swift river, you seem to sail with the bridge very rapidly, but you do not move at all. The river that does move, casts a shadow movement opposite to itself. When you shake yourself, and take a positive stand saying, "I do not move, and the bridge does not move," you will stop with a sudden lurch, or else come slowly to realize that you are motionless.

So mortal mind, which is the moving law of opposites to realities must be told that none of its statements are true. There is but one mind thinking thoughts. That Mind thinking good thoughts. Thus the mind that thinks evil is no mind at all. Either we come up suddenly from sickness, sin or stubbornness, when we say this, or we are slow to realize its truth.

It takes some resistance on our part against sense evidence, to believe in the statements of science, but we cannot make them of practical benefit, till we do take this stand and hold it. We must do the will, before we prove the law; that is, we must speak the Truth. If we suffer doubts, we must struggle past them by such efforts that it seems as if the conscious and unconscious mind must dissolve with the intensity. "Let the waters be gathered together unto one place, and let the dry land appear." Effort on our part, effort of separation; "the natural mind perceiveth not the things of the spirit." It must be driven to acknowledge them.

All who make the effort get new experiences. If we say there is no matter, we lose sight of matter and its power. If we say there is no sin, we feel one with holiness, we purify all things around us. If we say, "God works through me to will and to do," all things we then do will turn out to be the wisest things that could have been done in bringing Truth in its saving power to light, and the conviction of this grows to be intense and comforting.

If we say, "I am governed by the law of God," we feel one with stern, inexorable uncompromising law itself, and that law holds us against sin. But these passages of resulting experience preceding fitness for work, are not intense at first, they are light. As we go on getting nearer to that fitness we long for, they grow more wonderful, and new light pours in.

When we are perfectly prepared for the highest work we are expected to do, we shall give off potency, and do the great work of our Father without effort. If it is the healing we are to do, our presence will heal, so that wherever we go, healing virtue will flow through us, the result of our mental conviction of the non-existence of disease and sickness.

If it is sin we are to conquer, the Truth itself which we trust in, will convict every one of sin in its presence, and people will turn from the error of their ways just by association with us, even though we say but little. This is the Science of Silence, or the systematized knowledge of the laws of silence, as power.

Self training is a silent process. You must tread the wine press of salvation alone. The bringing to pass upon yourself in body or mind, or new conditions, is silence. When the silence does break over into words that can be heard, they carry all before them, but only the trained mind can speak words that are sure to convince or heal suddenly.

When we have set our whole being aright, by conscious thoughts, we are vivified with power. We set out with words that seem preposterous, that we cannot ourselves prove. Other people can prove them, but they seem nonsense to us, this is doubt. We show our youth in the Science of Life when we are forcing ourselves to speak its laws.

We cannot prove death as nothing, and prove sickness, which leads to death, as nothing, till we have entered the path by the right way or gate. It is very humble, cold, tedious work to set out with.

We are often asked if we cannot take away some of the ruggedness of the first lessons of Science. No, only a sudden pulling up of our minds to face the bold, discouraging Truth will attract attention.

Pulpits and teachers have tried to lure people in with soft words about matter being reality, and evil such a dangerous thing that they had better get inside the warm folds of theology. But the world had got discouraged at the long delay of the good things (the heaven they promised) and refused even to listen to them. We must seek the way, and knock at the door of the Good Kingdom with the right startling words, till it opens to us. We must argue by holding the conscious mind or intellect to the Truths of Science, from the sway and surge of wrong beliefs and indecisions.

We harness the intellect to the service of the true self which speaks the Truth in science, in the face of everything that opposes, till we become convinced through and through of the truth of our utterances, and the concentrated conviction of dry land of our being is formed, vivified, determined, built, prepared to bring forth life as the resulting potency of conviction. It is the speaking into recognition, or awakening into manifestation, of the intuitive faculty, the spiritual principle in us, of which all metaphysicians in all countries have said, — If there only could be a way to awaken it, it would give man dominion over his body, over the powers of his mind or intellect, over the arts and sciences, over nature, for it is one with the Origin or Principle that gives body, mind, arts, sciences and nature, being.

"Let the waters be gathered together unto one place and let the dry land appear." Always "let there be" shows duty on our part, or as in the text — Let the next steps follow, a moving up and on. This always comes after a trial of faith. The conscious mind determines anew to hold this Truth, and the unconscious mind is moved on, or changed a little. For as we think, so do we show forth by our screen pictures or magic-lantern views of ourselves, called physical bodies, the body standing in the same relation to its mind as screen does to the picture in the camera.

After my trial of faith, when I am determined that "Neither height, nor depth, nor principalities, nor powers, nor any other creature shall be able to separate me" from that which saves, I seem to go on a little, and the change is pictured forth on something that for convenience, and by common consent, has been denominated A PHYSICAL BODY.

All who plant their minds in the determination to stand firmly to the scientific statements which work such results, report bodily changes following their thoughts. Sounder judgment comes, and improved health conditions. Either slowly or quickly, affairs of daily life begin to improve. But this will never happen while we are depending upon external agencies for help. While we lean upon material aids, as upon glasses to see with, upon visible medicines to help our bodily health, upon crutches, canes, ointments, liniments, we put off the day of faith. We put off the day of power. We put off the day of understanding of the principle. Then we wail and wonder why health does not come to us and our families! Then we marvel why we do not bring symmetry to deformity, wisdom to foolishness, and happiness to misery.

Half the time, people who wonder why they fail to carry some important case, are those who believe they are told what to do by some psychologic influence, not by Truth itself. These influences are not to be trusted; they are false. They are in the realm of mortal mind. To get your full growth you must swing clear out of them and their teachings.

There is no work you cannot do, believing in Truth. Truth is a silent principle pregnant with power, you speak it into an action that puts old conditions out of sight. You speak the still forces into action, into life movement. All changes for better date back to the time when Truth, spoken by some conscious mind, either your own or another's, set your conscious mind to work aright.

Persistent insistence of any truth by mortal conscious mind, will set it into harmony with Truth.

One who works hard to solve a problem in mathematics, but cannot get the right calculation and result, will if he labors long enough, set the mechanical action of the brain to work, and while his conscious intellect is asleep or roving elsewhere, the action of calculation will keep up, and by and by, get the answer for him. Psysiologists call this "unconscious cerebration." Health can be set to coming in the same way, by persistent thoughts setting toward health. Happiness can be brought to our hearts, by persistent use of right words. Poverty can be turned into riches by the same strong thoughts, sight brought into manifestation by the powerful thoughts of truth. Intellect can be intensified to brilliance by the same determination.

These changes are external pictures of the new establishing of mind on a new basis, by the volition or willing of mind to be true, which awakens the spirit of Truth.

Socrates, in the *Phaedo*, tells of the deceitful reports of the senses. The soul, which in this connection, means the conscious mind or psychic soul, should withdraw from them, for to listen to them brings belief in them, then sickness, waste of property; and trust the Principal will work for us or with us, when we have spoken it, will set it to work sooner, and make it show forth quicker. But every time we say what is true, even though hot quite believing it, we have commenced the change.

We say, "God works through me to will and to do," and our work begins to change its kind and quality. We begin to be expected to do things we had never dreamed of. All the old plans we had made, and the old work we had done, seem to have been getting ready to come into this service. All that we have ever learned or gathered, all our culture, our accomplishments, or genius, are useful to us only to convert people from supposing that things are true and real about themselves which are not true and real, from supposing that they can get satisfaction in the ways they look for it. Then by and by we become such radiators of Truth in its strength, that we do not take on falsities or weakness from other minds.

People who are exceedingly sensitive to praise and blame, people who are made ill or weak by other mentalities, are not fully in the Science, no matter how much they claim that they are. They must grow to such a strength that no one can darken or shake them.

Characteristics of error must be washed away by denial. Pride, deceit, treacherous or cruel tendencies must be washed away by the erasive potency of denial, just as disease is washed away or erased.

Sometimes we are afraid other people will get our places from us, or make us of less consequence than we want to be. Such thoughts keep us from healing ourselves and others. We are overborne by the mortal law, and not masters of it. Cast away pride, state that you are not proud. Sometimes we resent other peoples' doings with us, or the hand of fate. Deny it. We must not let resentment of mortal mind conquer us.

We cannot break the chains that seem to bind us, to compel us to look at shadows in a cave (to borrow from an ancient myth), till we strike them off by our word of denial or destruction. Thus are sins washed way, errors of judgment or suppositions laid down; thus sins are remitted and for them the new character is given.

"Create in me a clean heart, O God, and renew a right spirit within me."

Now note: In science, sins are washed away by true rendering; errors are denied, and forgiveness comes. That is, for error you have truth given. And this is repentance, turning from error to Truth; and this is washing of sins away, denying their reality, making them nothing; and this is forgiveness, giving for mistakes, Truth. When the sinner begs for forgiveness he wants his sins made nothing by the blood of Christ. Now blood means word, and Christ means Truth. Thus he really wants the word of Truth.

When character is established, or mind is made firm on this basis, we become fit soil for all these seed thoughts to spring up for the sustainment of others in need. The evolution of the race from error, is the salvation we are commanded to accomplish, and teach, and preach. God works to do that necessary thing, and that only. We shall see it as we go on.

We will often find ourselves working apparently to no purpose; that is, the results will not be quickly manifest. We have to keep right on. We must talk on the side of Truth. It is the side we think on, talk on, that shows forth on the body and our work. Our own words vivify our silent energies. That is, what we purposely think and speak, fills us with convictions, and such convictions as we hold in the mind, are what strikes out and touches other people.

The words we speak or think are instantly shown by the blood; and the settled convictions that we have formed are shown by the fleshly organs. So the skillful practitioner catches your state of mind, both conscious and unconscious (that is, what you now think and what you have thought, and what other people have thought and now think about you), and he deals with that as the cause of your disease.

Nothing evil that comes up must be admitted true. No murmur, no complaint must escape our lips, no mention of sickness, weariness or pain. Everything that is spoken in our presence, we must mentally deny, if it is evil or undesirable. Every time we stop on our way to admit sickness is true, we have compromised with evil, and are in a degree rendered powerless or weak to destroy the evil we have fellowshipped with; we have become its friend and not its foe.

All evil asks is that we acknowledge it. It counterfeits the demand of Good. The denial of evil, sickness, sorrow, poverty, etc., mentally kills it. It bruises the serpent's head. To say it is real, makes it show as sorrow sickness, giving it local habitation and name.

Now there are other things besides sickness and sin that can be denied out of existence by our word. If we are in poverty, trouble, anxiety, name the state or condition and deny it. Wait a little for the effect of the word of denial, and then say that the blessing we want is ours already. According to scripture, "Pray as if you had already received the blessing." If you are in seeming poverty, deny poverty, and affirm your rightful and true supply. Science denies the evidences of sense every time, and about everything.

In *Science And Health* we read, "Rely not in the least on the evidence of the senses." Jesus the Christ said, "Judge not according to the appearance, but judge righteous judgment." That is, according to reason.

To stand firmly amid the breakers of poverty, sorrow, desolation, wronged lives, age, sickness, deformity, and say, "None of this is true, only that which is Good and True shall come into my life," — to stand firm in these statements, is to see the old past die, and a new life open.

If I were sorrowful because someone has wronged me, I would say, "That is not true, there is nothing wrong. No one can do me an injury, or wrong me in any way. If I am unhappy, or sorrowful, there is no law of mortal mind that can make me believe that which is not good. I am glad and joyous, happy and free. God is my defense and comforter, my shield and from the suppositional evil, and by His marvelous law all these things that I have said are true will surely come to pass, as I have thought, so hath it come to me."

Conscious thinking is working. And "my words shall not return unto me void, they shall accomplish that whereunto they are sent."

Thus it will be seen that we are responsible for even our environments; for all the circumstances and conditions that surround us; and thus it is that being our brother's keeper, he who came to the world and saw the needs of the world, and recognized our responsibility for the complications and errors into which we had fallen through belief in materiality, said, "Preach the gospel — heal the sick — cast out demons (evil thoughts or propensities) raise the dead. Those dead in trespasses and sin, save them from the mortal (carnal) mind; make then spiritually minded, so that the time may come when all shall know Good, from the least unto the greatest, and they shall not need, each man to tell his neighbor — 'Lo! here is God, or Lo! there' for 'Even upon the bells of the horses shall be written holiness to the Lord.' "

Thus through faith, or the determination to hold steadfastly, comes peace or stability of mind through stability of mind vivified by the of Truth, comes power to decree; and thus the children of understanding establish true law; and thus comes power to do the work that lies around us waiting, which is our commanded work, bringing balm to wounded minds, health to sickness, gladness to sorrow, freedom to bondage, rest to weariness, strength to weakness, riches to poverty.

"All that man calls the world, is but the picture of his thought."

To be subject to such laws as ignorance has made, is to believe in, and be subject to no law at all. If we hold out against the good and true as ALL, we build the walls of delusion closer. That is, if we say anything evil is true, we build a wall of darkness. We must press past these walls by stern rejections.

Decree to come to pass the good things that you desire. "Thou shalt decree a thing, and it shall be established unto thee, and the light shall shine upon all your ways. When men are cast down, thou shalt say there is lifting up. And he shall save the humble person."

Think truly, and thy thoughts

Will the world's famine feed

Speak truly, and each word or thing

Will be a fruitful seed,

Live truly, and thy life shall be

A great and noble creed.

No matter if you fail to bring these things to pass in your own time that you have set. No matter if the great outside world *seems* to slay your law. No matter how slowly you work. Sometime it shall come to pass; while you are yet speaking, the answer will come.

"Though wrong grind thee small, and all shine ends defeat, yet shall the world grow polar to thee, slowly taught, and crystal out a new world like thy thought."

# LESSON SIX

## Thought Transference

Now and then, as you listen to the teachings of Science, a new thought flashes through your mind, and a sudden understanding of its meaning comes to you. Then you accept it gladly as a truth newly revealed, or you say, "It is too good to be true!"

These flashes are spiritual understanding. By the degree that you experience recognition of Truth, you understand it, and by the degree that you understand any principle, you are one with it.

These are flashes of the vivifying Principle which makes the young words you set out with in practice effective — able to show forth in the external life, or body, of the sick minds into which they are sent.

The careless mind thinks any kind of cure good enough. But while we are in the way of cure, we will take the best.

On the principle of thought transference, whereby one mind can make another hear, although no audible word be spoken, any patient under treatment will mentally hear first the word that erases from his mind the false conclusion about himself, and secondly he agrees gladly with the new thought calculated to give him health. This is particularly true of diseases whose causes do not lie in guilt of conscience. By this I mean, people are quickly and easily appealed to by mental argument when the belief of disease simply is to be removed; but when the disease is the outward symptom of some secret fault, the patient does not readily let go the cause which lies back of the symptoms, and so recovery is slow.

To remove the causes in character, we must understand mind, which makes character.

Does not mind make character? Does not a wrong habit or an evil trait originate in a motive of mind or some voluntary choice, as that one *thinks* falsely before his character becomes deceitful? Does not one choose in mind to oppose his friend's tastes and wishes, before he gets stubborn of character? Does not one choose to possess the things that belong to his fellow-beings, before becoming selfish? Does not one choose to wound a loved one's heart, before he says the contemptuous, the scornful, the sarcastic word that by-and-by makes him an unendurable companion because of continual ill temper?

Well, these characteristics are the immediate causes of most diseases of mankind. They bear a scientific relation to them.

We are now speaking of mortal mind. Every point of evidence given by mortal mind is diametrically opposite to Immortal Mind. That is, where mortal mind says death is, Immortal Mind says life is. Where mortal mind says sickness, imperfection and material formations are, Immortal Mind declares wholeness, perfection and spiritual things to be. Now because Immortal Mind is Truth, therefore, all these other claims stand as error to be rejected or denied.

If the error in a mathematical problem is not pointed out as error, and erased, it claims to be true, where only the Truth is true. So in mortal mind — which is negation of Truth, according to Science — its statements are the claim of the lie, always opposite to the actual. And because all its statements are opposite to the actual, we are able to deny them, or reject them on scientific principles; and by the strong statement of what is actually true, we make the true thing visible.

As the writing of invisible ink comes out clearly when exposed to heat, so when your true word is sent upon the mind of your patient, the white sun-fire of Truth with its actinic ray — your understanding — brings out in bold, legible characters called physical health, awakened intelligence, purified motives, the very words which you have put on the receptive and absorptive mind of your patient.

Unless we shiver and thrill with the loss of consciousness of the mortal, and the free movement through us of the Immortal, we are not in understanding sufficient to heal quickly that patient whose own secret faults lie as the cause of the cancer, the swelled joints or the nervous derangement. Neither can we heal ourselves quickly.

When thus themselves at fault, practitioners of mental healing may sometimes be heard threatening to declare the Truth a lie, or to denounce it as a fraud! Sometimes they get to a point where, instead of putting their trust more and more in Truth, they trust it less and less — simply because the erasure from the body of its diseases does not result quickly. They do not see that this is the trail of faith by which the Law tests every mind — either establishing its firmness thereby, or letting it, by its own choice, resolve back to void or ignorance again.

As has been already said, idiopathic diseases, or those caught by contact with different minds, are quickly cured, on the principle of the receptivity of every mind to thoughts of health when transferred to it from another mind. But symptomatic diseases, which slowly lift their hydra heads from secret sins, do not yield save to the swift fire of understanding.

What you *understand* never leaves you. What you believe because others tell you, may slip from you.

If your power to heal grows less and less, gradually failing you, it is probable that all you have done of healing was on the plane of thought transference to minds not suffering from guilt, but innocently deceived into their condition by mortal suppositions. It was not accomplished through or by reason of understanding of the Health Principle.

What is this understanding upon which so much depends that with all our getting, we are enjoined to get it — for it is life, and health and peace — and whose not having is possible wreckage of our power to go forth and heal body of its unfailingly?

Every mind looks toward understanding as the goal — the ultimate of its hopes and ambitions. It is the nature of mind to look toward this goal and ultimate, as it is the nature of the planets to turn toward the light of the sun. But the mind that attains to this has sprung the bounds of intellectual processes, and entered a realm above and beyond intellect, where thoughts, formerly powerless, are suddenly imbued with potency to achieve results beyond the conception of mortal mind.

Understanding is the gift of God to his children as the reward of faithful reasoning in the name of Truth itself, for the help and salvation of our fellow-men. For, according to his talent, each of us, must compel his conscious mind or intellect to use its faculties for the highest service, and with the highest motives, before understanding will vivify his words with vital energy. That is, the ultimate toward which mind hastens can never be reached till every faculty we have is directed toward service for Truth, by calling forth the best of our fellow-men in bodily health, in character, in intelligence.

We can tell how to seek understanding, we can tell movement of it, and its marvelous influence upon those who come into its radiance as it flashes through us. But to explain *it* is to explain God himself, for its every flash is a ray from the Most High Intelligence. It is for us to declare its movement — the mysterious exercise of its law; but as the wind bloweth where it listeth, and thou canst not tell whence or whither the principle of it, but only that it is — as we know the working of gravitation, but not the hidden secret of its power — so with understanding we may know how to get it, and know the blessedness of its having, and know the effect of the moving thereof — but we do not yet know its intrinsic nature. We can only name it, and tell its workings.

In order that you may desire understanding above rubies and all riches, you must be told about it — you must be shown the necessity for it in Mental Science. Then in whatever rank and file of life you place yourself, you will be able to know exactly where you stand, so that you may not talk against the Science, or fail to use it, on account of any lack of knowledge as to just where you belong in it.

And first: If you do not persistently *use* the foundation principle, its argument and application, — you have no right to talk about understanding it. For no one can have anything better than a mere intellectual apprehension of the Truth, who does not prove it by demonstration. No one can understand the Science of Life till he has spoken it to help others — to teach, or heal, or otherwise practice it for the world's salvation.

Understanding is a spiritual awakening that strikes through, and shivers with white heat all the faculties of mind, taking the intellect by the hand, and guiding it into the meekness of a little child, or harnessing it like a docile steed to its service.

No one can claim understanding of the Science who yields himself to obey the control of another being, less than God himself. "Thou shalt not bow down thyself to them" — that is, yield to any — "nor serve them" — which is, obey any. To get under the dominion or control of even a Solomon or a Socrates, living or dead, is to deteriorate; because, instead of letting the light of your own self shine as you are commanded, *you* are lost for the time being — are his to whom you yield yourself servant to obey. Understanding will not shine through you. You will get white-faced and sodden, and no radiance will flash from Omniscience to make you fresher and more powerful, healthier and more beloved. Seek wisdom from *Truth* itself.

It giveth liberally in reward for faithful service of telling it daily — silently or audibly — telling it! telling it!

Do not claim that you understand Truth's service, if you still lean on material drugs — compounds — glasses, canes, crutches, pills, surgical operations, or appliances of any kind whatever to make you or your fellow-creatures whole and well, or to enable them to help themselves more effectually. Truth is uncompromising. It will not divide honors. Many people who are interested in the Science, or even work for it, urging and helping others to understand, are still tampering with, or depending upon, material aids to health. They are still liable to suffering. Their diseases have not wholly left them. And they never will till the word of Truth alone is trusted to deliver and to cure. Cast *all* your care on it. "Call thou upon me in the day of adversity, and I will deliver thee." "And Asa sought not unto the Lord, but unto the physicians, and Asa slept with his fathers."

In the old days men sought for the elixir of life. The seeking — the desire — was *promissum* of the elixir's reality. Truth *spoken* shall open within you the well of living water springing up into everlasting life. The last enemy you are to overthrow in its name, is death. It is the fountain of perpetual youth which Ponce de Leon failed to find in fair southern Florida. "Thou shalt run and not be weary, walk and not faint," and "The beauty of the Lord thy God shall be upon thee."

The ancients sought the secret of transmuting all things into gold. To know that all is gold, or good, is the true philosopher's stone, putting a priceless value upon all things, making by the word, by and by, all things golden blessings.

"And God saw that it was good."

"God is Mind, and mind sees by knowing. Mind sees, or knows its thoughts, or creations, to be good.

The idea of Mind is a likeness of it — therefore it does a like work. Its work is thinking. This compels us, who are the idea of Eternal Mind, to recognize our work as good; that is, to recognize our thoughts as good — not as dependent upon material laws or conditions, but as coming straight from Eternal Mind itself.

This is the highest possible mental altitude, and changes all things to us.

We start out with speaking spiritual truths. We do not see them — understand them. But by and by we do understand. "The entrance of Thy words giveth light, it giveth understanding." This is unvarying law. Then we know good. Then we also can say — "My Father worketh hitherto and I work." And he establisheth the work of our hands, our strong thoughts.

Understanding is a spiritual birth. What we first know by the hearing of the ear, and accept because we can follow the reasoning somebody lays before us and are led by it to certain conclusions, is all very well for the time being. But this simple following of a line of reasoning, though it leads up to the desired mental state, is not itself final perception.

When we really and truly stand for the right, we speak of excellent things not as a duty, with teeth set and mind rigidly compelled, but with the joy and gladness of love. When people come whining and crying, and sick and discouraged, they are not in love with the Good, they are fellowshipping with the not-good, clinging to negation, to nothing at all, which is ignorance. People in trouble of any sort are followers of ignorance, of darkness.

But they who understand Truth Itself, and know their relations to it, are glad. They "rejoice because their lover is with them," and they are in the light. They love the Good and see it. They love it because they see it. They put evil conditions to one side with a breath of rejection, and turn the night of sorrow into the morning of joy by a single word of Truth flashed forth from the pure recognition of it. They turn disease into health by a shake of the head and a word of re-assurance.

But every mind, however great its claim of ignorance, must work toward the day of understanding. Whether by a quick spring into the light, or by slow, labored steps, is at its own option. It is written that every eye shall see. That is, every eye of flesh shall see that the flesh in all its claims to intelligence profiteth nothing — the Spirit is all.

Now in the state of its natural ignorance, flesh claims that its knowledge is worth having; that a knowledge of shadows — the worms and leaves, the stones and bones of material existence, are of great account. The spiritual life and its wonderful wisdom, deep unto deep of majestic lore, waiting in the silence for the word of recognition to call it forth into manifestation — the flesh calls foolishness. The mind of flesh — the intellect — calls spiritual lore foolishness. "The natural man perceiveth not the things of the spirit, for they are foolishness unto him."

But the mind of flesh — the intellect — is that with which we first hear the word of spoken Truth. And the way and march of intellect from misconception to perception — from misunderstanding to understanding, is growth into recognition and obedience of Spirit. Losing itself in service of its Master. Night losing itself in light. It is swinging out from the dominion of the old knowledge that profiteth nothing, into the new wisdom that profiteth with power and joy.

Swing inward, O gates of the future!

Swing outward, ye doors of the past!

For the word of the true thoughts is moving

To bring light that comforts at last.

And this on-going — this process of the loss of intellect in the light of spiritual understanding, is our own experience every one. For our help in this evolution, for our aid and instruction, our calling into the true way, our leading — even the stones and sums of the material world are given us as pictures of the way from void and uselessness to definite form and perfect usefulness. A description of any one creation from the heart of the great invisible Silent Principle into manifested or proved reality, is the description of all things.

The story of creation as told in the first chapter of Genesis is the history of a thought of Eternal Mind coming forth from the mother-bosom to proof or manifestation of itself. It is a symbolic picture of the mind of humanity proving its divine origin, — its destiny and office.

All the thoughts of God are clear and excellent to their Thinker. Their springing forth in creation only means that they must prove their nature and office to themselves and to others. This is called manifestation — revelation. "There is nothing covered that shall not be revealed; neither hid, that shall not be known."

We, as thoughts of the Most High, have for our office the revelation of ourselves. And this revelation is the process with which we have to deal, the problem which we must work out. The creation itself is the reality in the mind of its Origin. The making manifest, or showing, is our work — the work of our thought. We are the thought, and "without it, (thought) was not anything made that was made."

The original mind creates. We — the likeness of that Mind — do a *like* work. Not *the* work of creating, but a like — the image of reflection of the Real — the *seeming* to create, which is not actual creating, but only the making manifest of that which is already created.

The child of Good is in nature and office perfect. But he must prove this. When he has proved it to himself, he has entered into understanding. When he proves it to others, he does so by showing perfection of character, and power in work — by his power to prove others also good.

When a patient comes in illness, unwhole — unholiness — to be made over into health — wholeness, this wholeness or perfection is not created by the healer; it is only made manifest. The real self is never sick. When an appearance of sickness shows forth the real self is not visible.

No point is so difficult of making clear to the learner as this. What *is* this thing that appears to be a sick body? Is not my leg — my arm — my head, a real leg — arm — head? No! The real hand is absent from view, is invisible. There is in the invisible actual a divine reality, a perfect substance, which all the visible material things but stand for — shadow forth. But in no sense, even when most perfect, is any physical organ or any physical object anything more than a sign that there is a true, substantial thing near, though unseen?

The true substance is the true mind of all things; the "Divine Idea" of the ancients. Its thinking faculty is pure understanding This substance casts a shadow. This shadow is intellectual belief. So wonderful is understanding that even its shadow, belief, has itself the power to shadow forth a belief, and this belief is called flesh! It is a belief which has no actual existence in itself, but only shadows the actual, casts a sign of it.

To speak either audibly or mentally of the real self, is to make it show itself. The real self is absent or present to belief, according as the believing power — that is, mortal mind, declares. If mortal mind declares a sickness, sickness shows. If it declares health, health shows. But that health which is not declared from the mind that is grounded in spiritual understanding, is not the health which cannot be broken. It is only the belief of health, not the understanding of it.

Sometimes wicked and unprincipled people have sound bodies and strong intellects. They are good types of the infinite variety of mortal mind's beliefs, and showings forth of beliefs. As one star differs from another, so does every mind differ from its neighbor-mind in the kind of belief it reflects.

Over the waves of mortal mind come beliefs in conditions, which beliefs are passed on from one mind to another. Whoever gets the belief that health belongs to him, will appropriate health. Whoever catches from another mind the belief of sickness, is sick. Either belief, however, is not based in knowledge of the law of mental action; therefore, either belief is liable to be shaken. When he knows that health cannot be taken from him because he, the true self, is never sick, then only is health secure.

When the fleshy declares health to be the manifestation of the Spirit's perfect presence, then it cannot be changed into sickness. *No power whatever* can quench the light of this understanding, nor weaken the arm that is empowered by the strength of it.

But the fleshy, (which by all its showing as matter, is not the real — being negation, *not* Truth) standing alone in its own weakness, believes what is not true. So it believes health, which is wholeness — which is holiness — which is God — can be destroyed. He who believes health can be destroyed, believes God can be destroyed, for God is The All. The All is Wholeness — wholeness is Health (wholth). God is the health of his people. "Acknowledge me" — "Prove me now." "And shine health shall spring forth speedily."

I, in the flesh, must see God; you, in the flesh, must see God.

That is flesh, which is the shadow, must know itself as the shadow — the unreal; must declare itself nothing, and must give way to Soul. When the flesh declares — "I am nothing, thou art all, O Spirit!" — then a change begins to come to pass in the mind. Ignorance disappears beneath the light of this truth, as a shadow grows less and less as the sun rises into midheaven, until, when it shines directly overhead, the shadow is lost utterly in the substance — the real. Where does the shadow go? Where does the ignorance go? It is lost in Truth. And with the loss of the shadow — the ignorance is lost also. The miserable tumor, the vicious rheumatism, the ugly dyspepsia — these, themselves the shadows cast by ignorance, are lost with their shadow-father from which they had emanated. "Ye are of your father, the devil; he is a liar, and the father of it."

Evil conditions are but the proofs of ignorance, and when that goes, they, too, are gone.

It is the lesson of most ancient teaching that when one knows that the actual Self of him is indestructible, unchangeable, never yielding to imperfection, he knows all that he need know. That self of him has begun its office of proving its excellence, and soon will put the shadow of itself, so that as shadow, it is lost in the beauty and perfectness of the real substance or its true self.

Hufeland, body physician to the King of Prussia, agreed that "the real self, which is what we do not see, is never sick and cannot be sick."

To speak of this perfection, is to begin to prove it. Health sets in as a first sign of spirituality.

All physical things are the semblance only — the outpicturings — of things not yet shown. "For now we see through a glass darkly, but then face to face."

Then if matter is but the unreal semblance of the real thing or entity, it is easy to say matter is nonentity; and nonentity is nothingness. Why then be troubled by the logical conclusion — the statement that physical things are nothing?

The whole business of the real self is to show itself — to make itself manifest

As a shadow is grotesque, distorted, when the sun is low, so is the physical self when it does not acknowledge Truth. But when the sun is in its zenith, the shadow is lost. So when Truth absolute is spoken of ourselves, the physical lets go its claim, and the spiritual shines over and through us, and around us, glorifying us and all things to us. "The mortal puts on immortality."

"Let your light shine" means, let your true self stand forth by telling Truth. You need not be always preaching and talking aloud, and thus exhibiting zeal without judgment; but your silent thought may shine and flash its excellence over the presence of the joyless and sick, over the people in the streets of restlessness, over the disheartened criminal in his cell, the cruel-hearted, the over-bearing and dishonest among the swarms of mortality's roving children. Send them your silent word: The vile and wrong are unreal! Only the good is true!

Do you see yet what this service is that brings understanding?

Just speaking the Truth, one way or another, for the purpose of proving evil unreal, and good real.

There are many ways of speaking the Truth, but they all lead the mind up toward its desired goal — Understanding. They must all have for their end or purpose, the making of others to know the Good. We must help on the millennial day — that one day when "all shall know Me from the least unto the greatest."

We may speak the Truth for the purpose of making people healthy and strong. We call the way, healing. To practice healing by the silent speaking of the Truth will lead us to understanding. "Heal the sick."

We may write about the Truth for the purpose of making others wiser and happier. This, too, being a form of teaching, will lead us into understanding' "Go ye into all the world, teaching and healing."

We may preach the Truth by declaring its general principles aloud to multitudes, or by expounding it carefully, bit by bit, argument by argument, to classes met for instruction. By this way, also, we are led into understanding, whether they to whom we have striven to bring the great message will hear it or not. "Preach the Gospel."

Spiritual understanding is the light that illumines the pages of Scripture. But it does not come to us, till we have faithfully worked for the Truth. Understanding, which is wisdom, cannot be bought or sold. Weeping and begging will not give it to us. It is the reward for faithful service.

People complain that they do not understand the Science. Have they worked to deserve under standing?

What work? Worked how?

Have they, with the word of their speaking, silent or audible, rejected the claims of mortal mind respecting their fellow-men and themselves, till all evil and undesirable conditions are as blank to them as to Swedenborg's angels, to whom only the good of each being is known? Do they speak only of the true and deathless excellence of life and mind, or do they fret at the misery and folly so visible to the children of darkness? "By thy words thou art justified, and by thy words condemned." "Call no man your father, for one is your Father, even God." Declare yourself the child of the Good. Persistently think of the divineness of your birthright. "As a man thinketh in his, heart, so is he." By and by, life will be all joy and wisdom wheresoever you go.

Perception of *good* is understanding of Law.

Perception of Good, which is understanding, never comes clear to us, nor makes potent our effort, till our persistent word of Truth has had its sway with us over and beyond all temptations to speak of foolishness and evil. In a moment — in the twinkling of an eye, when the rubbish of false beliefs is cleared away by the wonderful word of our speaking, the True flashes its reality and beauty before us. "Ye have received the Spirit of adoption.'

To think about the real self of you when you think of yourself; to think about the self of your neighbor when you think his name; to speak to this self mentally is to call it forth and to make it shine over the poor fleshly representative.

When your friend does a wrong thing, it is not himself that does it at all. It is the false semblance of him — the spurious, counterfeit, imitation.

Call to the self of him! Cry aloud in the deep silence to the Real Self!

This sort of service to the Truth brings you into union with the Christ — into at-one-ment, brings you into the same mind that was his — *at-one-mens* — at one mind. "Let the same mind be in you that was in Christ Jesus our Lord."

How shall we get the same eternal Mind which he called the Father speaking through him? By speaking the same words that He spake. "It is the Spirit that quickeneth. The flesh profiteth nothing." "Ye are the children of the living God."

This is the blood of Christ. Blood is the symbol of life, and blood is the outward showing of conscious word, silent or audible — silent or audible conscious thought. "The blood is the life," saith Scripture. And "the words that I speak unto you, they are life." The blood of Christ means the word of Truth. "Drink ye all of it." That is, accept my word.

We must be washed clean of our old belief in evil by the speaking of this word of Truth. Then we shall find that the Christ hath indeed atoned — that is, that Truth has rewarded us by making us one with itself by the blood, or true word.

When people think of the physical state, they are thinking of and calculating about nonentity — mere negation. As we are always like that which we study, the study of negations dulls, paralyzes. A negative state is a sleeping state in the law of symbolization. "Awake! thou that sleepest!" cried Paul. See how sorrow benumbs you — see how cheating hardens you — see how deceitfulness dulls your ability to read other people's motives and character. Sorrow would not benumb you if you could shake it off your mind. You would not cheat if your mind did not covet your neighbor's property. You would not be deceitful, if you did not first consciously wish to make people believe that which is not true. Thus thinking wrongly, falsely, foolishly, negatives us — dulls, stupefies, darkens us.

According to mental physiology, when we dream in our sleep that we have gone to sleep, or dream anything about sleep, we are then on the point of awaking. So, with us who are in this negative state, or dreaming state of mortality; when the flesh acknowledges that it is the nothing, the negation, the dream, and cries, "I will awake, arise and go to my Father!" — it is then that we begin to stir with the new life of spiritual understanding. There flashes through us a ray of Divine Light — the reward of the words we have spoken.

Arise and sing of the True! Shout! Oh, daughter of the Good! "Then shall thy light break forth as the morning and thine health spring forth speedily."

Then new powers vivify us. New interpretations of Truth come to us. We read Scripture with a new insight into its meaning! Formerly a sealed book to our understanding, it opens treasures of promise and prophecy whose true blessedness the old interpreters have never revealed.

We learn that all Scripture is the statement of Immortal Mind's procedure first, and mortal mind's on-going second.

Take the book of Genesis with which we are now dealing. The first chapter tells of the true and real creation of God. The second chapter gives the shadow of that creation — a so-called creation by the Lord God. This is not the real, but the unreal — not the True, but the untrue — not the Immortal, but the mortal. The Lord God in the second chapter is the law of the shadow — the Law of Truth as portrayed by untruth.

God created his child to have dominion over the world, making him so excellent that he pronounced him very good, and setting him over all things of the land and sea and air. Yet in the after creation of the Adam-man, or error-man, this very dominion is declared null and void because of imperfection. But the seeming law of the Adam-man or error-man and his world is determined by the true law, or law of Truth. As the statement "all is life" makes the correlative statement "there is no death" imperative, so the statement, "the all is the true creation" makes essentially right "the nothing is the false creation."

We say that, as Spirit, we are the children of good. Then as flesh, we are the children of evil, "prone to err as the sparks fly upward." "Ye are of your father the devil," that is, the evil.

We say we are the children of Wisdom. We hear the command to seek wisdom — to knock at the gates of it. But the Adam-man or error-man is told that he must not know good and evil. The tree of the knowledge of it is forbidden to him. The true child says — "I had not known sin but by the law;" that is, — I had not known what is not good unless I had first known and recognized Good. But the Adam-man knows neither Good nor evil.

Thus the law that all *is* the Good, is the very creator of its visionary converse, the law of seeming evil — that is, of what would be if Good were not omnipresent. He who stands at the portals of being, as do all the children of men, is given power to see the law. The law is realized by mind. Each self is the I. Each of us should know that the I of Him — the self of him — is mind, soul, spirit, intelligence, like unto its Origin — Creator, Father.

We know the law of Substance and thereby the law of shadow. If we keep our mind on spiritual things, the kingdom of heaven, which lies right here, though invisible, is all open to us — glory unto glory — joy unto joy — new revelation unto new revelation! But if we look only at the shadow, we see things opposite indeed to the kingdom of heaven. We see the law of death — the unreal.

The unit one, looking forward to ciphers at its right, sees added value into value. But looking toward ciphers at its left, it sees diminishing value, down — down — down to the remoteness of infinitesimal valuelessness. Yet always the diminishing value results from its opposite. We say one million when we look to the right — one millionth, looking to the left. Unless we first understand the million by looking to the right of the unit, we can never understand the fraction at its left.

So we cannot know the law of shadows, till we know that the substance which casts them.

So we cannot know what the flesh is, till we understand Spirit.

So we are told to "seek first the kingdom of God," which is the invisible kingdom revealed by righteousness — that is shown by right thinking — and then "all these things shall be added."

If we turn to the right, we then know the sign of right. We declare for Spiritual Truth, and all things begin to be signs of good at once. Poverty is turned into plenty — misery into happiness. We ignore the shadow and turn to the substance. Then, for us, all is true substance.

For to say — "misery is a lie," and to add "the Good is true — is ALL" soon makes God show.

Now, the, people begin to query — Do you mean that a murderer's act is a good thing? No! But the self of him is absent to our belief; very absent. Looking down the way toward death by the shadow's distorted difference, that which we think we see is not really true; it is an ugly dream. Call to the self of him! He will turn, and the nightmare is broken. The wicked hand drops. The deed is not done. Swedenborg says the man who is hung opens his eyes and finds he was not hung. He finds that he never committed the crime. The sufferer finds that he never suffered. It was mortality's ugly phantasm.

So all temptations are suddenly no temptations. So all evil deeds are found to have been but ugly dreams, from which, however, we never awaken till the Reality is declared.

Now, are you supposing that the evil-doer may get consolation to himself from his evil deeds done?

Not so. While any belief in evil exists, suffering accompanies it. When one yields to temptations to evil, he is as the child of darkness — of supposition — of belief — mortal mind; and he must take the consequences of the beliefs he fellowships with. Punishment is the unvarying result of wrong-doing, in the realm of mortality, where he supposes himself to dwell. All these things are the transactions which *would* be, if such a realm were real.

Error, or shadow, seems to be real. Hence it must be met and dealt with as though it were real.

You say 5 and 3 are not 6. That is, you name the error, and by so doing you prove it good for nothing.

Well, so you name another error, flesh, and say it is nothing, has no reality. You tell why flesh is the shadow that declineth, and name with positive distinctness what is real substance. Never till we call all flesh and all matter as it appears, the unreal, and boldly declare Spirit, which is invisible, as all — just as Jesus of Nazareth did, saying, "the flesh profiteth nothing, Spirit is all" — can we begin to prove to others and to ourselves how divine we are in origin.

That is, we cannot otherwise prove that the kingdom of God, which is the kingdom of all that we desire, is right here within our reach, as declared by prophets and seers, and by the first begotten Son of God, our elder brother.

How well Paul understood the light that begins to shine over all who give to old things their newly translated names. "Giving thanks unto the Father, which hath made *us* to be partakers of the inheritance of the Saints in light, who hath translated us into the kingdom of His dear Son."

Where was that kingdom of the Son into which they were then already translated? It was the new mind into which they had come. It was the recognition of what is real, and the naming of that which sensation says is real, by its right name, NOTHINGNESS.

Into that kingdom we may enter while on earth, — or while to others we seem to talk and walk and sleep — and deal with affairs exactly like the people who do not believe; "In the world, but not of it."

The Egyptian Balthazar, being made to speak a thought that has run unchanged through the centuries whenever the devout have opened vision to things of the Immortal, said, "There is a kingdom on the earth, though it is not of it, — a kingdom wider than the bounds of the earth, though they were rolled together as finest gold and spread by the beating of hammers. Its existence is a fact, as our hearts are facts, and we journey through it from birth to death without seeing it; nor shall any man see it till he has first known his own soul; for the kingdom is not for him, but for his soul. And in its dominion there is glory such as hath not entered into imagination — original, incomparable, impossible of increase."

Yet we may see it. We may speak of it till it dawns upon our sight. For we *may* know our own Soul.

Then we are like transformed ones, for we have gotten a taste of the wisdom of the Mind that is God. Then we understand, and look, talk and act more spiritually.

People watch the shadow cast by their belief — that which they call their body. They see it go through changes. They say it is born, it experiences, it dies, and perhaps lives again in a more serial form in a new kingdom. They wonder and marvel at it. They talk of its changes. They never seem to be quite satisfied as to its final disposition — what becomes of it. Of course not! Bodies are only shadows of belief; and what becomes of shadows?

These people are as if they watched a cloud-shadow in summertime. We look down upon the grassy field and see a long shadow flitting over it. We say — Oh! see that long strange shadow! How queerly it acts! We give chase to catch and examine it. But it is gone! If we had looked up at the cloud itself, we should know why the shadow disappeared. The real cloud has ascended, or been absorbed into the sun-rays. If we watch the cloud we can see what becomes of it; we can understand its movements. We are not so baffled and discouraged by them as by the shadow and its doings.

Now *we* are a ray-flash from the Mind that is God. The name of ourself is Soul — Understanding — Mind. We as understanding, cast a shadow. The shadow of understanding is belief. Belief casts a shadow. The shadow of belief is flesh and other material things. Belief watches its own shadows and says they do strange things. The longer it watches them the more puzzled and baffled it gets. But when belief knows that they are but as shadows, and then declares the true that Substance or names it, that Substance, which is Understanding, shows forth as *judgment faculty* in the place of belief.

Then, when we understand, we know the Good. We are at one with it by a state of mind. And this is the atonement — the at-one-ment, or one mind, of the Science of Mind. We are partakers of the atonement when we have understood that all is Mind.

Then we are lifted above the ills and miseries of daily cares. We see the great world slip by us and say to all things — You shall know only the good to me — You shall work only blessedness to me — You shall be servants to do good to all the children of earth.

While we are outside this recognition that there is but one Mind, of which we are each a thought, there is the belief of homesickness and wandering and restlessness, even in the mind of the most prosperous and successful. Understanding is rest. Belief is restless, and the shadow of belief, body, more restless still. Restless people are absorbed in thinking about their body, or some pride of the heart, or ambition for selfish greatness.

Raymond Lully, born in Majorca, in 1200, said, "There is nothing the mind so longs for as to get reconciled to, or one with God." This is to get into harmony with; and to get into harmony with, we must understand; for we are like that which we understand. Thus understanding of mind is atonement. Men think it is houses and lands and power and learning they need to satisfy them. But no. None of these things will satisfy. On the death-bed they moan with terror, or tell of their eagerness for reconciliation with the Eternal Mind.

The gifted and much admired Margaret Fuller said, "I am deeply homesick; but where is the home? If not on earth, why should I look for it elsewhere? If I cannot make a spot of ground yield me the corn and the wine of life here and now, famine may be my portion forever and ever, surely."

Though you may have plenty of money, you may cry like the older Vanderbilt on his death-bed, "I am poor and needy." He had lived all his experience here, supposing that true satisfaction consisted of holding material possessions.

Though you may have physical health if it is not founded on the knowledge that God is your health, any day may see the ignorance of this vital truth picturing itself upon your body as rottenness of bones, decay of sinews, inactive and enfeebled lungs, liver, brain or heart. It is the law that ignorance of Truth is pictured as disease. The law of negation hurries all its creations to the end of negation's claims, which is death. Every step of the way of its going, it is opposite to the process of Reality.

One cannot learn by studying the negation itself, any more than by studying the movements of shadows on a wall without seeing the objects that cast them. Such observations could be carefully made, and calculations therefrom laboriously classified and labeled. But they could never be depended upon, because the objects that cast them would move on, or change their relation to the light. One who studies the rocks and the stars, taking measurements and basing theories thereon, may return to renew his studies after the absence of a day, and find everything changed, so that his work must all be gone over anew.

Though you be wise with the learning of the schools, your head stuffed with the lore of the Brahma Somaj — the prick of a tiny needle, or a pebble from the hand of a baby, may take all this information from you by destroying the brain in which you trust.

Do you not realize this?

Emerson, the greatest ethical teacher of our country, lost his intellectual vigor before he died so that memory of law and logic, friends and events, slipped from him. On his return from the funeral of Longfellow, he said, "That was a sweet soul just passed on, but I do not now recall his name." He who had known the law of guidance through lowly listening at the doors of Silence, had not himself obeyed the law. Once he had said, "God is omnipresent, or He is not. He is all, or nothing." But he would not stop to reason out the scheme of his own being, and its possibility of good, from that postulate. If he had, the divine soul of him would have come manifestly forth to prove its health, which time would only have made more sweet and beautiful; to prove mental vigor, which years would only have brightened; to prove peace, which the turmoil of days could not have disturbed from its stately repose.

Of what use, then, to know history, art and science, if these upon which we depend for our happiness may flee away and leave us stranded without them?

Hear the verdict of the greatest scientist in the realm of the material universe who ever lived. "Knowledge that profiteth not" and "vanity of vanities — in the grave whither thou goest." Yet he knew of all growing things, from the cedars of Lebanon to the hyssop that springeth on the wall.

But knowledge of what is real — the true Substance — can never be taken from you. Moth and rust cannot corrupt. It is true and deathless, and laid up forever out of the possibility of destruction.

As a mirror declares what manner of face you have, so Science, in telling you constantly of the true Substance, the ALL, tells you of yourself. You study it, and become like it. And when the thrill of Understanding shivers through you, then you are bound to the Divine Mind.

It is the *re* and *ligo* — the re-binding, the re-union and reconciliation of your mind into harmony with the Mind that is God, after the disjunctive agency of sin (error) has been annulled. This is true religion — true atonement.

You prove this existing union by declaring it — acknowledging it. Let the shadow of understanding, which is mortal intellect, call spiritual understanding its substance by positive insistence. Then it flashes down into all your ways, and you forget sorrow and misfortune and littleness.

People say of the materialists that they seem to have no souls. They are supremely selfish. They are cruel. They have studied the soulless — the shadow — the belief — the opposite of soul — and they are absent from understanding. But let them look up from their stones and bones and acids, and think: "All these things are but the signs of a world invisible!" and lo! they begin to freshen; Soul begins to shift over and through, and they begin to grow more tender and thoughtful, more sweet and deep.

Agassis was like this. At the last he acknowledged that all these wondrous natural objects of which he knew so much are but signs only of something invisible — the world a shadow of the true world about which we wonder and speculate with the mortal mind, until we come to understand and enter spiritually.

All healing, as I was taught, depends upon our recognition of God as the Good, and of ourself as its creation only — which recognition is understanding, whose bright hot rays conduct us over the bogs and morasses of sorrow, despair and illness, destroying them as we pass. That is, as the understanding of Truth comes, beliefs in the lie are put out of mind.

But understanding comes only with work — which work is the telling of Truth.

All misery is a sign that men are trying to get satisfaction from wrong channels. Remember this. Satisfaction out of negations — nothings. It can never be found along this line.

Some think that to please the senses is the way to be happy. Some think that knowledge of trees and gases and anatomy and languages makes happy and satisfies the end of life. Some think money will do it. But all these lines of endeavor give restlessness. Yet the world is still trying to get proof *in* the flesh, of the Good — is trying to make Good real *to* the flesh. And this is the push of the law, it *will* prove to error that it is error — to flesh that it is flesh, and therefore profiteth nothing and Spirit shall shine ever and extinguish it.

The sun *will* rise overhead to dissipate the shadow — to lose it in the thing that cast it.

Insight into the unity of the mind of man with the Mind that is God, is the profoundest knowledge possible to obtain. It is the opening of prison doors. It is joy forevermore. It *is* the wisdom. It is the one only knowledge that profiteth. But knowing this, we know all things. All things lie open before us. All things can be accomplished.

"Wisdom is with him that hath understanding." "And they that understand among the people shall be wise and do exploits."

It is found by our declaration of it. It is made potent to us by our naming of it. We enter into union with it by understanding it, and understanding comes as the reward of service. The service is fourfold: Healing, teaching, preaching and living the word.

The day is at hand, and now is, when a Science of Religion will be reasoned out treating of the relation of the finite mind to the infinite, and of body to soul. It will be taught in the new church that shall guide and control the coming ages; in fulfillment of prophecy. It will at first be unwelcomed, derided by the strong laws of the sciences in vogue and favor; but with heaven for its beams and rafters, and its foundations set into the rock of Everlasting Truth, it shall stand unshaken. All who enter in at its gates do so by their own choice. Whosoever will, may partake of its Word. And the Word will lead to sweet peace all who speak it. The word of it which we speak is the Comforter promised, which shall lead into all Truth. Therefore, "Apply shine heart to understanding", for "My words are life unto those that find them, and health to all their flesh."

# LESSON SEVEN

## Baskets of Eternal Food

Many wishing to remember all the points of the lessons, and finding that they do not, begin to be discouraged, fearing that possibly they cannot learn all that is necessary that they should know in order to become Christian Science practitioners.

It is as if we should get discouraged because we could not eat everything upon a well spread table. We appropriate what is convenient for us, and assimilate what the system is capable of assimilating for regular working material.

The lessons of science are twelve baskets full of eternal food — the bread and meat of life. We need not strive and struggle to receive them; simple willingness to accept the Truth when it is spoken, and a healthy eagerness to use it wisely, is all that is necessary, to make us storehouses of plenty, the best of teachers, and the best of workers.

We do not have to try to remember the points of the Science. They remember us. They are alive with intelligence and love. They never leave us nor forsake us. They are like Swedenborg's wise angels, who meet the children of earth when they reach the next sphere. With tiny delicate instruments they lift the drooping lids of the eyes that are not strong enough to bear the light of the more ethereal realm. If the sight is still too feeble to bear the brilliance, they go away for awhile, but return again and again, till the eyes are become quite equal to the glory of the new day. The angel messenger never leaves the newly arrived one till his eyes are fully opened to behold all the things of the heavenly kingdom.

Swedenborg was always seeing symbolic movements. Science explains how his vision should be interpreted to show the workings of Truth, by ideas and words spoken to enlighten the mind. The ideas return again and again, like the gentle angels, and with the very words we first heard, lift at last the curtains of darkness, "Till we awake in thy likeness, O Truth!"

The sixth lesson is a face-to-face treatment, to train intellect to the gateway of understanding. The mark of it never leaves him who once hears it. There is a living, breathing quality about spiritual teachings that tinges the mind with vital colorings, which, once given, cannot be washed away — ideas which, once heard, can never be destroyed. They will set the seal of their meaning deeper and deeper, till you understand them, till you are one with them.

Many not knowing that the words of Truth have this living quality, feeling anxiously eager to remember and comprehend everything, but finding themselves unable to do so, wander from book to book, and from one expounder of doctrine to another, to be helped into understanding of these principles. They fall in perhaps, with enterprising talkers, not at all suited to help them on, being less spiritually awake than themselves, and are thus run back into old theological interpretations again, or into theosophy as incorrectly taught, and then the principle of these lessons works slowly.

What should they do, you ask, if they feel themselves to be floundering in the dark? *Work on what they do know*, and keep silence as to the rest. If they talk about being in the dark and not understanding, they will get darker and more like the "not" they talk about. "By thy words shalt thou be justified, and by thy words thou shalt be condemned." When the earth gets an impetus toward darkness, it plunges into its midnight. When the mind thinks of ignorance, it gets more ignorant still.

There is but one little point essential to remember and it is so simple that no one need ever forget it. It is that conscious mind makes all unconscious conditions, so that we are always showing forth a body such as our thoughts used to be, or such as are the thoughts of somebody else with whom we have associated. People sometimes speak of conscious and unconscious as positive and negative. Of course, they are talking in the language of mortal mind, when they speak of positive and negative or conscious and unconscious. We ought to be trained in spiritual laws, so that it would be given us to quickly name the thoughts that have made the conditions of mortal mind.

The mental vision can get so quick and sharp, that mortality's ways are laid bare before it. No one is so hard to deceive as the persistent student of Truth. We ought to be able to see and intercept the very thoughts that are now forming the future conditions of disease and immortality. Ordinary vision is slow, and sees nothing till it is actually thrust upon it. That is, we do not see the disease coming on, but only the disease come. We do not see chicken pox on the child's face, though photography may depict it as already there. The sun seems to be still on the horizon's bar to our physical sight after it has already descended below the horizon. A bit of fire on the end of a stick twirled round and round, gives circles and bars of light, but there is only a tiny point of fire there all the time. This is called "persistence of vision" in the schools.

Persistence of physical vision is a symbol of the persistence of mind in holding to old ideas. Physicists say, Why not admit physical cause and physical effect? — for certainly the persistently apparent is more reasonable than the unseen and imaginary, and everything shows physical causation. But the wisest students of pure physics have been an endless time studying physical causation, yet they pathetically look up from their investigations to report, "The ultimate cause is invisible!" After running conditions down to molecule, monad and atom, they are puzzled to discover where molecule, monad and atom originated.

MORTAL MIND CREATED THEM, says the Scientist, and spiritual law annuls them.

But still the wise heads are shaken at mental causation, and with the persistent clinging to old ideas, which persistence of vision symbolizes, they keep on studying physical causation, and feebly wishing, as Lionel Beale expresses it, for "something to upset natural law."

Remember it is somebody's conscious thinking, that makes every unconscious condition. It may not be the sick person's own conscious thought which has thrown the picture of illness upon him; it may be another's. The unconscious reports to the conscious, after it has been set going. The sun warms the earth, and the earth reports its heat to the enfolding atmosphere.

A certain set of metaphysicians claims that the conscious mind envelops the unconscious, as the atmosphere enwraps the earth. They speak of it as the "oversoul." The "over-soul" or "pure con-sciousness," makes and unmakes all visible conditions, or what we term bodily, or physical conditions. We may make our own or others may make them for us. This is enough to know of the ways of mortal mind to set out with. All the rest comes to us as we go along. Mortal conscious mind, often called the "psychic soul" with the conscious mind, which is the body, or visible showing it makes of itself, troubles the young scientist greatly, because so many good people have called it the real self, soul or spirit. If it were the real of us, then the Real is a very imperfect creation, for this psychic soul makes a miserable lot of bodies, and shows itself a very poor thinker indeed.

The real self is perfect, unerring, divinely wise. All its thoughts and actions are perfect, like unto its Creator. It is the image and likeness of its Creator. It makes the Spiritual body, totally unlike anybody seen by mortal eyes. "It doth not yet appear," because we have not put mortality away. *Let us put mortality away.* Deny its reality.

If you have followed out the line of Scientific reasoning at all, You must have discovered that you are gifted with powers and privi-leges you have heretofore little suspected. The knowledge of this awakens new impulses and new desires. These desires generally lie very near the fleshly or earthly conditions as thoughts of health for the body, food for its sustenance and comfort for its senses. So exclusively have these considerations occupied us hitherto, that when by con-scious mind we first determine to throw all that we are into the service of the spiritual or real self, for it to control, we are still closely enough related to our fellow beings, to care first and foremost about their health of body, its sustenance and comfort. So that our greatest desire now is to help the sick and poor and sorrowful out of their fleshly bondage. These are divine ministrations, and there is a way provided for the feeblest among us to heal and comfort and uplift.

In looking at the physical body from the metaphysical stand-point, we take the conclusions of students of mental action in relation to bodily conditions, that there is nothing in the physical body which had not a prior existence in the mind. This was Swedenborg's doctrine of correspondence, and he made a great study of the kinds of thoughts that produce special functions and organs. Some have attempted to explain that the lungs correspond to wisdom, and in size, characteristics and constitution, indicate how wise or foolish the man or woman; that the heart's size, constitution and conditions measure our capacity for loving; that the bowels, in their peculiar varieties show how compassionate their owners, and so on. As if by a species of statics and dynamics of organic function and functional performance, the mental capacities and capabilities could be weighed and measured. And these organs in disease are supposed to represent the abnormal or unnatural mental states which they stand for.

This doctrine of correspondence could never be made a science, because of mortal mind's subtleties, whereby the unamiable characteristics of one child showing out as diseased liver, may be exactly like the characteristics of another, showing as nervous exhaustion. All mortal mind's statements are error, and as it can never be calculated where an error of any kind will lead us, so no system of correspondence could ever teach us what error is certain to end a certain way. We can only learn to name the errors as they present themselves and scientifically erase them off the board of human experiences.

Every patient that comes before us, is a child come with his problem solved according to mortal mind's teachings. The calculation is all wrong, and he is hastening down toward death by the way of disease. He wanted to solve his problem so as to live and be well, but he trembles with terror because he sees that the entire work is wrong, and the conclusion false. He has never been without the true schoolmaster. "The light that lighteth every man that cometh into the world" How earnestly all students of real life and spiritual laws have insisted upon this! But mortality has kept five voices perpetually disputing its silent laws.

What has mortality told each child of flesh? At every point of statement you may be sure it has informed directly contrary to the truth about the *self*. It has tried with all the subtlety of error, to start at the foundations of being, and to follow in a semblance of orderly going, with a series of false accusations against the child of the Most High.

These false accusations formulate the seeming, the opposite to the real self — the fleshly.

The demand of our patient is upon us, that we evolve from the invisible, the true self, as the light is evolved from within darkness, by the agreement of our own enlightened or truly awakened mind with his silent, REAL SELF.

Now the sameness of procedure of all evolutions, from invisibility to manifestation, holds good in bringing forth or evolving health from unhealth.

The stages to recovery, or coming health, are invariably six, before the seventh or settled excellence is established. It makes no difference whether the progress is slow or quick, the stages or changes are six in number. The seventh is health secure. "Commit thy works unto the Lord, and thy thoughts shall be established."

When the stages are slow, they are perceptible, and we can study them, and are obliged to meet every change by a changing word — an impetus giving thought toward health complete. If you can read these changes, you are spiritually wise, and will know what word to give to hasten the desired manifestation of health. "A right word, how good it is," "Behold, I bring health and cure."

But there is a rule of health that works it into view, just as there is a rule in mathematics by which to demonstrate every principle. The simplest mind can learn this rule, and by its application work out health from unhealth, even when so untrained in spiritual perception, as not to be able to detect the errors of mortality as shown upon the diseased body.

There are three modes of cure in strict Science, adapted to the three kinds of mind the Scientists are characterized by. The first is the highest state of mind — pure spiritual quality, when the spirit beareth witness that we are one with it, and does the work for us while we are practically unconscious of being even instrumental in the cure. We are only conscious of a divine willingness to help our fellow being, and certain of the presence of a Helper who can do all things.

The second is that power which they feel who know whereof they speak and are keen-visioned enough to see what special opposition to Truth lies as the foundation cause of the sickness. They strike the sharp ax of denial at the root of the matter, and never stop striking till the tree is laid low and Truth springs up with healing in its leaves.

That is, they strike out the basic lie which created the disease and plant a truth there which shows forth as health. Denial is the sharp ax. All error waits the destroying efficiency of denial; "Lies wait and cries earnestly for extinction."

The third and lowest or commonest state of mind is the mind too untrained in mental action to read its claims, but honestly eager to aid in restoring suffering humanity to health and happiness. More of us are in this state than any other, and most of the healing done over the country is accomplished by these faithful, simple hearted children of the Science.

The faithful over the few little points of in formation soon grow to be rulers over the many, for it does not take the stupidest of us long to rise to keen reading of the states of mortal mind and influences that make them.

The child using his rule faithfully soon works rapidly without his rule. And persistent dealing with his principle sometime makes him a master of the use of it. So with the seemingly prosy dull rule of health, we soon spring the rule into quick judgment, and from quick judgment to oneness with the Principle that heals, is spiritual quality — the most blessed gift of God rewarding faithful service.

Sometimes the stages toward health are so marked and distinct that the use of the regular rule finds response. That is, each treatment takes the patient just one step toward health. It is a wise student who sees that some treatments push the patient ahead several steps.

Some conditions are simple and one right word covers the whole need. "Who can measure the force of a right word." Therefore the skilled practitioner and the encouraging teacher tell young workers in healing to "look instantly for the salvation," as sometimes the simple word "NO" acts like magic to what has been thought an incurable malady, driving it away in the twinkling of an eye.

But for the most part poor humanity under the decrees of mortality is subject to the regular race errors with respect to personality, and needs the whole rule of health given it, "line upon line and precept upon precept." So when you come into the presence of sickness and disease, you may be sure of certain things you can say in the silence which have sure healing potency. Knowing the universal false beliefs of the natural man with respect to himself, the order of their appearance, and their effects, we may feel safe to try the healing rule upon the very, worst malady these beliefs can result in.

I will now tell you of a severe case of so-called rheumatism that yielded its hold day-by-day in response to the rule of health repeated in the silence. I was young in the practice, of healing and not advanced into faith and understanding sufficient to heal by realization that the work was already done and nothing was expected of me to prove health to be the only reality. I had often been told this, to be sure. The best practitioners with whom I was daily associated often told me that *nothing was expected of me, but to realize that Spirit was the only presence and health the only reality*. But as with the rest of young strugglers into spiritual life, this was all strange language to me. Had I not previously been a student of ethics and life laws, how I should ever have got on with mortal mind's presentations while realizing nothing whatever of spiritual verities, I do not know. But the five voices of mortality were familiar to me, and the progress of human life from birth to death a common argument against the goodness of God.

The young girl, my patient, had suffered in belief for years the wearing full pain of rheumatism. Doctors and liniments and poultices had failed to help her. Someone sent her to me to be treated by Christian Science. My heart went out in sympathy as she described all this, and I felt certain that I could not help her; in those days I was not steadied by faith, nor inspired by understanding. The longer she talked the more real her malady seemed and the more incompetent I felt. Instead of standing boldly erect like a sturdy oak in the wind of her positive statements, I lay low under them, like the young trees and grasses of early summer. The information that her ancestors had all had the same complaint was overwhelming. Had I not known the ugly tenacity of inherited traits, according to the mortal mind beliefs of "heredity?" How could my feeble word meet the race-law? Suddenly the memory of my teacher's words concerning denial, recalled to me my judgment. No! I said in the silence. Then at every statement she made, I firmly said, No! which I tried to match with her positive absorption of interest in herself and in her experiences. She was like most patients, absorbingly interested in her own body. They always draw the unpracticed or unspiritual mind into their own quality of despair and fleshly belief.

Great courage came to me with the denial of her condition. I remembered certain things I had learned. One was that, the eyes of every human being tell the story of his life. Behind the suavity of speech and manner that would deceive the very elect with its semblance of sincerity, lies the character which the eyes reveal. Eyes murky with treacherous dealings. Eyes muddy with thoughts of low bodily gratifications. Eyes bleary and sodden with temptations always yielded to. Iris mixed with the pupil, telling of many a trait unknown to the outside world — telling of appetites and passions not yet swept out of the temple of existence. Sometimes the eyes of the slighted and unloved children of men, look steadily into ours, clear pupils, shining like the Mithra-fires, beacon lights of a clear conscience. Age does not dull the soul light of sincerity, nor make muddy the waters springing from the bed rock of integrity.

But in no way was I shrewd enough to discover the characteristics of my patient by any glance into those heavy eyes. I was as blind as anybody could be. But the courage came with saying, "No" to her description of her sufferings.

As her problem stood, it was her belief in the result of environment. First, heredity; second, race laws; third, influences, direct or contagious; fourth, the law of cause and effect, or results of personal thoughts and actions; fifth, the special effect of direct intercourse or communication with single individuals.

When she ceased speaking of her ailments, I kept silence, I called her silently exactly as if I had addressed her aloud. "Every one He called by name. " "They had names written on their foreheads."

"Listen to me, I said mentally. At first, it did not seem as if she heard me. *The fact that a thought can go from one mind to another, and become the thought of that other mind*, I could not yet realize. Of course, I had read of the laws of the transference of thought, which the Abbe Frethim, Cordanus and Cornelius Agrippa had taught. But not till we see the effect of a strong thought sent forth, do we actually realize that there is an absolute law of thought transference, whereby the mind receives thought impressions, as the tympanum receives sound impressions.

I spoke to her again; suddenly I felt as if her mind responded in some mysterious way to my call, and I continued, addressing my thought directly to her listening mind. "Not one word of all this you have been telling me about yourself is true. You are not suffering from a malady called rheumatism. Now listen to me for what I tell you is the Truth.

"You have not inherited the consequences of the lustful passions and sensual appetites of your ancestors in a disease called rheumatism." Notice how I turned the heel of denial upon the head of the serpent, that had wound itself at slow length from birth in the flesh to threatened death. Degenerated tissues, watery, acid blood, was what mortal judgment named the serpent that threatened her, and through whose subtle influence she looked upon life. If I could turn the head into the dust, and crush this crowning result of the basic error of mortal mind concerning personality, I need not try to hit at the minor errors whose sum and substance make up the body of error. By this I mean, I need not name the rest of the sufferings she had spoken of, these are sure to die if their head and governor, rheumatism, is killed.

"You are not suffering the consequences of the lustful passions and sensual appetites of the race, you are not subject to the race laws of reflected conditions."

"You are not suffering the consequences of the lustful passions and sensual appetites of the people you associate with, in something you call rheumatism. You are not subject to the mortal law of belief in contagion. God, Spirit is free from contamination. You are spiritual, therefore you are free from the evil effects of sensual thoughts about you."

"You are not suffering the consequences of your own lustful passions and sensual appetites in something called rheumatism, you are not subject to the mortal law of cause and effect. All this that seems so real is delusion, the delusion of mortality. Spirit is free from the bondage and conditions of flesh and matter; therefore you are free."

We must bear in mind that all mortal conditions are errors against Truth and await denial. And the denial that is efficient must strike at the error which originated the condition. Every voice of error that whispers, tells a history of ongoing that must result in disease of the flesh it formulates. If there is special guiltiness of the mortal self, in thoughts unmet, then no denial we can make strikes so hard at the error that has built the disease, as this denial of self guiltiness.

I now refer to the special effect of individual association; the patient was with me then, and nobody's errors had at that time so great an opportunity to set the old conditions fast into her own mind as my own. It is always the opportunity of the last associate of it, so that the truth spoken or thought can destroy its whole history at any instant. We might be so charged with the light of truth that the darkness of error would disperse instantly when we came into its presence. The fact that I had not cured her the very first moment was evidence that enough mortal error of her own quality hid my light to fix her own gloom deeper. There was but one way to set her free from my own share of the mortal error of lustful passion and sensual appetite. Denial!

"You are not suffering this condition you call rheumatism because of reflecting lustful or sensual thoughts from my mind. You are hereby set free from such error in my character. Spirit is not darkened by mortal imperfection. You are free; therefore you are free from my mortal errors of whatever name or kind."

Like the mirror that shows likeness of every face before it, so is every mortal mind believed to image the one who thinks upon it last. I must take care that she reflect only the nature divine of my character. In only one way can be brushed aside my errors, and the truth be left clear and shining, — by the denial of their reality, we are not born of the flesh, and not subject to the result of such belief in sin, disease, etc. Denial will wash us clean of this.

"You are not diseased and sick. Disease and sickness do not belong to you. You are free and at peace. Because God is your Life, you cannot be threatened with death, no fear death nor yield to death. Because God is your health, you cannot be threatened with diseases, nor sickness, nor fear, nor yield to them ever. Because God is your Strength, you cannot be threatened with weakness, nor fear nor yield to weakness. Because God is your Peace, you cannot be threatened, with discord or in harmony of mind or body, nor fear discord or inharmony nor yield to it ever. GOD is your PEACE, DELIVERER, an ever-present help. There is nothing to fear. You are well and strong and at rest and at peace. Prove that you are well and strong and free from pain and discord, acknowledge to me and yourself that you are perfectly restored to health and happiness. Your own shall establish the truth that I have spoken. My words shall not return unto me void; they shall accomplish that whereunto they are sent."

Only the spiritually minded, the pure in heart see God.

He that is faithful over a few things, I will make him ruler over many.

Come and let us reason together.

Never tire of the earnest insistence of the invisible True.

# LESSON EIGHT

## Ye Are the Light of the World

"YE ARE THE LIGHT OF THE WORLD," said Jesus to those whose thoughts were shedding abroad the beautiful Truth he had told them.

"Be not deceived," he said, as if they would be sure to hear some plausible arguments against his definite teaching that they never were brought forth from the flesh at all.

"Call no man your father upon the earth, for one is your Father, which is in heaven."

"Let there be light," said Moses, trying to teach this same lesson of standing with the mind firm to Truth, while the arguments of error should be most plausible.

The light of Truth is the life and health and joy of those who come into its radiance.

Whosoever occupies his mind with thoughts that are true will heal and strengthen and uplift all who come near him. We shed abroad the character of our thoughts.

When Truth is the supreme theme of our mind we are life and health and peace to our neighbors. They drop their thoughts of death and disease and sorrow when we come near them or think upon them. It is the Truth that does this work. It is not the influence of our personality in any sense, if we are occupied in thinking true thoughts.

"THE WORDS THAT I SPEAK UNTO YOU, IT IS NOT I THAT SPEAK, BUT THE FATHER (Truth) THAT DWELLETH IN ME, HE DOETH THE WORKS."

All talk about any effects produced but by the beautiful ministry of Truth, is talk on the side of the negative, the nothing side. "Man can do all things with and for himself, but only one thing for his neighbor — give him freedom."

All influence exerted by one personality over another is mortal influence, or the effect of mortal mind — pure nothingness.

We should be above and out of the range of such influence. Even good people should not be able to urge us into any action because of our fear of them or affection for them.

Only Truth itself should stir us to action or change our mind from its ways of thinking. Only Principle should guide our actions. "I will guide thee with mine eye."

It is not possible for one mind to get control of another without putting that other under a ban of darkness and making it forget its birthright of freedom and power. To yield to personal influence is to confess doubt of God.

If we fear to displease people, if we desire to stand well with them if we dislike them, dwell upon their faults and failings, or are unhappy when we think of them, we are tacitly confessing that we are very much in error, "These were all deceived, being in error."

Mortal mind, through personality, makes us forget what is true of ourselves. It continually reminds us of evil and terrifies us with descriptions of the power of personal influence. It makes us forget how powerful we really are within ourselves, how wise we are of our own nature as the direct offspring of power and wisdom. "Remember now thy Creator." "I consulted with myself."

"As thy day is, so shall thy strength be." This is a great scientific truth we should never lose sight of. It means that whatever is for us to do and be, that we *can* do and be. We can do all things that belong to us to do. We can know all things that belong to us to know. We shall not be tempted above that we are able to resist. We shall have no illness or weakness but what we can throw off.

"All power is given unto me, in heaven and in earth."

The most ancient teaching known to the race tells us in another way just as Paul does. "Ye are sons of the Most High. Each child of the universe is a ray of the Infinite Soul, a thought of the Infinite

Mind, an offspring of Deathless Life. No fire was ever builded so hot that could burn him. No weapon was ever formed that could destroy him. No wind so powerful that could move him from his steadfast foundation. No sorrow threateneth, no imperfection lurketh, no destruction awaiteth. Fear thou not unto whom this truth has come for with the knowledge of it is the key to power and life eternal."

Carnal mind tells quite a contrary story. It surges over us with a great wave of insistence that this is not true. Through the influence of personality it whispers subtly that we are weak, that we are ill, that we are inferior — all pure deception. Judge not by feelings.

Some people know just enough of mortal mind to know its claims to power of influence, and just enough of Spiritual law to forget its defensive power, and so when they are weak, unhappy or ill, they are in great terror and mortal trepidation, instead of bold and brave with spiritual life and light.

They tell of being mesmerized, magnetized, hypnotized, psychologized, etc. and lay so much stress upon such conditions that they, being themselves deceived by belief in its power, deceive many others also.

Let us remember the power of Truth continually. Let us remember the word of Truth which declares that one true word may put a thousand errors to flight. Rise up and instead of describing the evil of mortality, declare the good of Spirituality: "I will not believe what is false. I will not be deceived into thinking I am less powerful than I AM! I will not believe in weakness or sickness for the child of Spirit! I am the child of God, therefore I am free, wise and strong. I do not believe in the reality of evil or matter. I do not believe that if God is Omnipresent there is any other Presence at all but God. If God is Good, then only The Good is Real. If God is Spirit, then All is Spirit.

"I do not accept the teachings of the best man or the best woman that ever lived, if that man or that woman says that God is the sender of evil, or permits evil in the universe.

"I reject anybody's verdict who believes in power of evil in any way or shape or fashion. I do not admit that it is possible for one human mind, call it by whatever name you please — psychology, mesmerism, hypnotism, animal mind, or whatever — to touch with trouble or trial one single instant of the life of any man or woman or child who has honestly confessed God as Spirit Omnipresent.

"I do not believe in poverty or sorrow or sickness. I know that it is unscientific to be poor or weak or unhappy. If I cry with trouble it is a falsehood against Good and in no sense a reality. If I am sick or weak it is a lie from the beginning.

"Nobody has any power to make me believe in the reality of evil at all. I think it is sanctimonious nonsense to be poor; and a certain conviction of false thoughts to be sick.

"I praise this wonderful Spirit present — this One Spirit — One Only — whom I adore and breathe my daily strength from."

Speak positively.

All the strange effects of personality are the counterfeits of the sweet influences of Truth. Reject them. To speak the words of Truth is to get changed by speaking. The very first words of Truth begin the change. The changes produced by Truth lead toward life. The changes produced by personal influence lead to death — to the nothingness from whence they sprang.

If the mind is weighted by calling material things real and true, deny that material things are real substance. This denial has the effect of unweighting us as if we had thrown ballast out of a heavily weighted balloon, or cut the cords that fastened it to the earth. Suddenly we feel dizzy or light-headed. Affirm the loving presence of God. The ground seems to slip from under us. Affirm that Spirit is the eternal Substance. If we do not eat — affirm that the word of Truth is meat and drink. We do not sleep. Affirm that we rest in God. We forget easily. "I will not forget thee, saith the Lord." We are like people who wake out of slumber.

Paul called the bondage to belief in matter sleep, and when he saw the people who had heard the gospel of Truth settling back into their old beliefs, again, he cried," Awake, thou that sleepest! Awake to righteousness, and sin not!"

Righteousness means right thinking, and sin means error of the mind; so he meant, awake to right thoughts, make no error.

No words in all the world will give the unweighting effect of denial of the reality of matter and evil. No words will sustain and satisfy like the words of Truth.

If we were in pain and groaning, and sorrow had weighted our hearts, and we should pray earnestly for the law that had smitten us with evil to make us submissive to its dealings with us, we should get the dulled, stupid feeling of one who has taken a dulling opiate. The dull, drugged feeling is the outpicturing of our prayer for relief which rose no higher than the idea of dull submission.

We always get exactly what we pray for.

What we believe in the heart or deepmost of the mind, is our prayer. If we think of submission as the gift of God, submission we will get. Life is a dull, hopeless affair to the one who has made up his mind that his God has sent evil upon him and purposes to keep the evil working.

Therefore the God that ye make you

Is grievous and brings you not aid,

Because it is for your sakes

That the God of your making is made.

Suppose that while you are praying for submission you are secretly and slyly longing for freedom?

You will be torn in the conflict of mental states, and consequently torn in the conflict of conditions that will come upon you.

Here is where the world seems to be. It is in chaos and discord. Its wise teachers explain with great and learned disquisitions that evil is necessary in God's plan. They preach that the sorrow and wrongs of the poor are to teach the rich generosity and pity, and that the injustice, oppressions and exactions of the rich are to teach the poor humility, patience and long suffering.

But the poor and rich keep singing. "The Truth shall make us free." There is a vague conviction in the race mind that Truth is a saving principle capable of emancipating us from evil conditions. We are called upon to note, however, that none of that talk about the beauty and blessedness of affliction frees us from them. None of the talk about the loveliness of sorrow and the goodness of poverty, supposed to be telling the truth, frees us from sorrow and poverty. None of it warms the limbs of the shivering, feeds the hungry, or looses the fangs of disease.

But notice; the instant we begin to deny the reality of evil, insist that pain is a delusions poverty is nonsense sickness is a dream, the senses are false, then we are loosed as by some mysterious agency from the whole lot of them.

If the words of denial strike out and take deep hold we experience their results marvelously. The very objects of the room seem to disappear. The people in it are forgotten. The pain that had such a hold upon us is none like the bits of the mad beast in our dream: "As a dream when one awaketh."

The debt that has burdened us, burdens us no longer. A strange lightness of heart takes possession of us. We suddenly remember that in this Presence are all the kingdoms of the world, and the riches of them. We trust to the "Friend that sticketh closer than a brother," to bring us help. And help comes after such a feeling of trust. Some blessed gift or unexpected success in affairs puts the money burden quite away. "Trust in the Lord, — and verily thou shalt be fed."

We cannot mourn. Sorrow flees away as on wings. The one who has wronged us repents and is good again. Good news from a far country, unexpected Joy comes.

All these changes are the result of speaking true words. No other words but these will lighten and brighten with practical efficiency. But we do not get perfect freedom till we throw out all the ballast — all the false beliefs. We cannot float fearlessly through Omnipresence, guided through its happy zones by the Motherhand of Omniscience, till we deny all evil things and thoughts. So, many students are always afraid of something. Sometimes they have been afraid of the results of speaking true words.

They have said boldly that they did not depend upon the brain for their intelligence, and then when they felt the convolutions of the brain move up, the gray particles change places, their memory going, they have been terrified, and thought that intelligence was going rather than coming. So they have clutched and struggled to comprehend mind. Now none may compass its ways. None may comprehend Mind. Mind comprehends us.

When strange experiences come we should rejoice, for Mind is working us up and over to be more like its eternal excellence. Rejoice and again rejoice at whatever experiences come, for "Thy lover is with thee, the Lord of Hosts is His name."

It was the whole aim of Jesus of Nazareth to raise the thoughts of his disciples above the sensuous plane to ideas of Truth, so he said, "Judge not according to appearance, but judge righteous judgment." Right judgment means according to reason. Right judgment compels us to reject the evidences of the senses in making up our conclusions about God and His creations.

Paul said, "We walk by faith and not by sight." Faith is substance — sub-stans — real truth known — a foundation over which the mind can walk safely and hopefully to the instantaneous fulfillment of its desires.

Paul also speaks of the righteousness of faith — the right thinking that faith compels, so often against the senses' evidence; so that we deny what the senses tell, and think good, true and beautiful things are real, instead of the ugly, hard conditions which the eyes, ears and feelings report.

The Kabalistic justice, the Sanskrit rite, Hermetic philosophy, Swedenborg — all teach the fallaciousness of sensation.

Schopenhauer declares that "he only is a philosopher to whom these things are distinct and certain."

But we do not have to quote authorities or study books in order to prove these things to ourselves. All we have to do is to make the Statement of Being and reason honestly from it to the next step. We see that if the Statement of Being is true, then what we see, hear, smell, taste, feel, so opposite to that statement, must be false. We therefore declare material claims false. Then we get the results of such declaration. We are unweighted of our old conditions in various ways; appetite is gone; heads are light; pain has disappeared; joints are loosened; sorrow has flown.

"Let us lay aside the weight and the sin that cloth beset us, and run with patience the race that is set before us."

"When I go away (as flesh) I will send the Comforter — the Spirit of Truth." Spirit of Truth means word of Truth. Speak it. Comfort, satisfaction, judgment faculty, new revelations come.

All these blessings have ever been waiting for our appropriation by speaking Truth. How silly all our former gropings seem to us now. Whom before we ignorantly worshipped, Him we now declare boldly. We now know Truth from error, "I had not known sin but by the (this) law."

All good blessings have waited our appropriation, and continually pressed themselves upon us by that law which has compelled all mankind to seek for what is good and best.

All religions and sciences, all arts and professions are making for the good of mankind. We complain of religion that it has not accomplished what we wanted. But its ministers have suffered martyrdom and exile, bravely trying to save mankind from the "awful power of evil."

We complain of medication — that its study has increased disease, and under its highest practice the greatest and best of our land "die in the, prime of life" as a tribute to its dealings. But what nobler martyrs has the world known than the brave surgeons and eager students of medication? They have "gladly laid down their lives" to prove to the world the mysterious laws of anesthetic and compounded drug, vivisection and dissection. Ardent disciples of Aesculapius have tried mortal poisons upon their own bodies and their families to show the healing efficiency of them. Arsenic, strychnine, opium, morphine, cocaine are permitted to paralyze and slay thousands that the few may demonstrate their power to live. Great and good doctors have exposed themselves to contagions and infections, "dying willingly by slow tortures" and carefully noting all the hard way toward death, for the instruction of others in mortality's ways.

"Why sought they the living among the dead?"

It is not culpability but race mistake that rests upon all these teachers. Right in the face of the Good at hand, and the incessant announcement of it by the inspired, they have looked to ways that would fail. Though they were told that, "The Lord is the health of His people;" "I am the Lord that healeth thee;" "Call thou upon me in the day of adversity and I will deliver thee;" "My words are life to them that find them and health to all their flesh;" "Speak the word only and my servant shall be healed," "Acknowledge me in all thy ways" — yet they would not heed. Though the highest light within them ever admitted the power and presence of God to do all things, yet sought they not Him.

The law of Truth is the true law shining within and around us all. The law of error is the false word whispering. "Let there be light," is the test.

We are all commanded to let our true light shine — "The light that lighteth every man." Over the bogs and morasses, into the valleys, down through the cold darkness of the deluded ways of the world, we are commanded to let the true word of Reason shine. And as nothing can withstand the chemicalizing, dematerializing, subtle power of the sun rays — from the drop of alcohol, that is lost so quickly, to the granite boulder which disintegrates in time, "till in me is matter's last gradation lost" — so nothing of error believed in can withstand the spoken word of absolute Truth. "Let your light shine." Speak the truth.

When the earth, which symbolizes mind, was in process of making manifest, the second step of its evolution was the making way for light, as the spirit of God moved across the face of the waters.

In our proceeding toward an acquaintance with Truth, we deal secondly with that word of Truth which brings light over the mind.

In our second bringing forth, for the help of others, we are to meet their second error in solving their life's problem. If they are in disease, as the crowning result of one special error, we can by denying the special error erase the disease. Of course we learn this fact as one of the first laws in the Principle of healing.

This had been told me repeatedly as a student of spiritual healing, about the time when I took charge of this patient I told you yesterday. I was continually trying to demonstrate it. But how to get at the special error was always the question with me. I could not be spiritually minded enough to see that she had been well and sound from the beginning and needed no treatment at all. The best practitioners daily explained to me that they denied the special errors of their cases.

Between the two ideas — nothing to heal and all to be demonstrated, I was at sea.

The girl who came to me so hopefully the next day after my denial of mortal mind's first error in her case, was not by any manner of means fully restored to health. She said she did not have the night sweat and had slept nearly ten hours, to her great delight, but she had been in almost constant pain since she arose in the morning, till she sat in the chair before me telling her experience. That moment the pain left her and she talked incessantly of herself and her surroundings, her inheritances and history.

There was a kind of hopelessness seized hold of me as she spoke. I felt as if I would give anything in the world if I had never heard of the Science with the awful responsibilities which knowing it brought. I could not bear to take money for treating her, I meditated, because I did not know enough about the Science, in its practical workings, to act the part of a physician and to be paid for what I could not be.

She began to tell me of Jane Brown, who had been arrested in _____ for failing to cure a case of consumption by Science. To be sure, she said, four doctors had declared there was no hope, and all they could do was to give the consumptive mixtures which they knew would do no good; but they had refused to grant a burial certificate, nevertheless, and poor Jane was under arrest for "practicing without a license."

Then they told me of Julia A., who had lost one out of her twenty cases of diphtheria, and the morning papers were full of condemnations of her practice. The nineteen well patients counted for nought — she was blamed severely for the loss of the twentieth. I had just read of a physician who had lost nineteen out of his twenty cases of diphtheria, and he was called a remarkably successful practitioner of medicine. I was quite depressed by so much whispering of evil. Suddenly I bethought myself. Always the true thought comes to everyone, as I have found since, and I am right thankful that I seized hold of it on that occasion. Not a word of all this is true!! I mentally exclaimed. *God is all! God is everywhere! I do not care what they tell me of evil. I will not believe it.* Then I began to say, *No!* severely, to all her communications. I did not hear them at all after that, I was so occupied in mentally speaking the word *No* as if I meant it.

When she ceased talking I understood that it was time to give a regular treatment. I felt much brighter and clearer. I could think quite independently. I could not help thinking over what I had read in the book, *Science and Health* about the true creation, and the beautiful statements which describe the making manifest of Mind or Spirit, with all its powers. Mind manifest as a creative Principle meets all the falsities of mortal evidence.

What error common to the race mind is the regular second error of mortality, safe to deny as having power to make the disease I am treating? I asked mentally of the Divine Wisdom so silently folding me round about. I wanted to feel some great revelation strike its white fire through me, such as some of the rest of the scientists had told of having. But no, all that came to me was this idea, which I was sure was right and true, as an explanation of what to speak in the silence.

It is evident that when we treat against the supposed consequences of being brought forth according to the laws of the flesh, and intimate by denial that it is sin to be so brought forth we do not mean sin according to the usual definition of the term, but only that it is an error — a mistake; that looking into the symbolization of things and processes as real, rather than knowing that these are not true and real but only mirages of the real, is error. In the world of seeming — the fleshly or earthly world that has environed our patients and made them what they seem — their second experience was the information coming from all sides, of the laws and processes and consequences of physical existence. These are the evidences of the senses as informed or analyzed by the intellect. Without intellect or conscious mind to determine, sensation is powerless.

The conscious intellect determines that things are true which are not true, insists that what can be seen by the eyes is real substance, and that the divine word of testimony telling perpetually against it is not the true word.

Now the conscious intellect is symbolized by the moon that lights the night time. The word of the real self — the law within us — the spiritual faculty — the intuitive perception — the divine reason of the mind, corresponds to the sun that lights the day, making all things plain.

It is the truth that makes free when it is permitted to guide, that heals from sickness, cures of sorrow and judges against the evidences of those senses which tell us that things may be wrong and unendurable in a world treated by the good, governed and occupied by The Good, and tolerating nothing but Good.

As the earth longs for the sunlight, so does the mind look for the divine light of Reason, the true word, to shine over life, making all things plain.

I had a memory of the great and good of earth who have traced the universality of this light within all mankind — this principle of righteousness, common to the race. Pythagoras called it the salt of man in all ages. Plutarch called it the inner guide. George Fox said, "It is an inward voice." Schelling said, "It is intellectual intuition." St. Bernard called it "divine sign" — divine self. John called it "the light that lighteth every man that cometh into the world." Paul called it "our school master." It always disputes the deceptive sensations. It disputes the power of personal influence. It denies all forms of deceitfulness. How brave and beautiful and perfect is this pure region within every life! My whole mind seemed to be concentrated upon this perfect Self and the child before me, ignoring quite definitely the whole appearance and testimony against its right of way.

I found myself saying involuntarily, *Listen to me!* She seemed indeed to be listening, in the mysterious way that Mind listens to Mind, and I continued; "You are not really suffering the condition called rheumatism. You are not suffering for inherited deception or deceitfulness. Spirit cannot be deceived. You are spiritual and you cannot be deceived into supposing that you have rheumatism or any other evil condition. The whole world could not deceive you into supposing you had such a condition. All the minds in the world are powerless to convince you of what is not true. You are free from race deception."

Just here I thought that I was really denying what so many of the scientists were denying so vigorously under another name. I was using the Bible term; they were calling it "mesmerism." I reasoned that mortal deception had been practiced long before Mesmer's time, and so "mesmerism" was really a misnomer for the process. Yet as the word occurred to me I added to my denial this statement so often spoken to me by the different worders: "You are not mesmerized by the race belief in rheumatism — not psychologized by a whole world of error — not magnetized — not hypnotized, consciously or unconsciously, into any belief in evil. Spirit is free forevermore. You are spiritual and free forevermore.

"All the people around you cannot deceive you by their believing in what is not true. You could not possibly be self-deceived into believing what is not true. Spirit is Truth itself. You are Spirit and Truth, one with this Presence in whom you live and move and have your being. You are free with the freedom of the Spirit. I have no power to deceive you into believing what is not true, and you have no power to deceive me into believing what is not true. We cannot deceive each other in any way, then, into believing that you, the child of God, have pain and disease. All belief in pain and disease is null and void, and you are now at peace with the peace of the Spirit. I tell you that because God is your life, you cannot be threatened with death, nor fear death, nor yield to death, ever; God is your Health — you cannot be threatened with disease or sickness, nor fear disease or sickness, nor yield to disease or sickness, ever; God is your strength — you cannot be threatened with weakness, nor fear weakness, nor yield to weakness, ever; God is your Peace — you cannot be threatened with discord or inharmony, nor fear discord or inharmony, nor yield to discord or inharmony, ever.

"You are perfectly well. You are free. You are Spirit. You trust God —"

It came to me that in some mysterious way I was quickening her mental faculties and calling forth from its hidden depths her power to trust in God, the attitude of mind I had often held when teaching children how to work out problems in mathematics. I would assure them so positively that they could work the problems. Then I would hold their fixed attention while I explained the why and wherefore of the whole process. Then I would call upon them to prove it all for themselves. I said to this girl firmly in the silence, "Prove that what I have said to you is true by acknowledging to yourself that you are perfectly sound, well, and absolutely free. Acknowledge to me that you are perfectly sound, well, and free."

By this time I was strongly charged with certainty of the truth of my words, and was not in the least surprised to have her tell me that she felt like a new creature — not a particle of discomfort in any part of her body. A wonderful lightness of heart had taken possession of her. She smiled into my face with a child-like confidence.

"My words shall not return unto me void; they shall accomplish that whereunto they are sent," I repeated in the silence, and then I quite forgot this patient in my eagerness to help the rest who came to me through the day, and to write an article for the little Christian Science Journal, as my teacher had requested. But when I looked over the names on my list, in the evening, I called her name and gave her the same mental treatment over again.

"Let there be light in the firmament."

"Wher'er the sacred rays of reason shine,

There dwells the God that utters truths divine."

"I am meek and lowly of heart."

# LESSON NINE

## Temple of the Living God

In Science we learn that spiritually we are "the temple of the living God." This knowledge causes us to show forth health and soundness in every way. People then tell that "their physical health is perfect, their mental perception clear, and their former tastes renovated." These "signs" following spiritual awakening cause many to investigate the Science.

The fact that bodily healing is accomplished by mental action is apt to make bodily healing seem of paramount importance to the young student of metaphysics.

But physical cure is only the natural and necessary outcome of full acceptance of the doctrine. Looking at healing for its own sake, all power to heal is liable to fail us, because confidence in the cleansing efficiency of the word of denial leaves us when we enter upon the denial of special sin, which is often the cause of chronic sickness. Sin may seem very real to one whose perception of the nothingness of matter is fairly good. "Cleanse thou me from secret faults." "Now ye are all clean through the words that I have spoken unto you."

When we are one with this doctrine, we can as readily negate the claims of sinfulness as of disease.

All who try to mix other doctrines with this one fail to cure. No one can serve two masters. No other doctrine in all the world will work with this one. No other doctrine teaches a state of mind or principle of action capable of erasing sin from the character and infirmity from the body. No. As at present taught, they all fix sin and disease into the life of the world as a God-permitted and necessary state of affairs.

To accept other teachings in full is to accept the teachings of Christian Science but in part. To accept Christian Science but in part is to fail to do the works of the Science. "Acknowledge me in all thy ways," is an imperative law.

Suppose your dearly beloved pastor is thrilled with indignation at the pernicious conduct of certain people, or condones with unscientific lenience their "evil actions, and you agree with him; then you have helped to fix the tendency into the character of the man you have been talking about, and are yourself a companion of his quality. You are comrade with that sinner whom you condone, and participator with him whose life you hate, because it is as much of a reality to yourself as to him. Then he comes to you for treatment. You and he are both walking the same road of belief. You are both looking through the same colored glass of prejudice. "If the blind lead the blind, they both fall into the ditch." So you cannot heal him, because his ugly disposition is more real to you than the words of denial you are speaking. Then, of course, you do not heal anybody as quickly as one who does not harbor the belief in the reality of evil at all.

Now the moment you do not heal as quickly as your neighbor, you begin to think that certain minds can send their thoughts with more effectual results than others; that it requires a special gift to heal, etc. As God is no respecter of persons, it is very unscientific to think that He will work more perfectly through one than another of His children. Unscientific thoughts concerning God are like leathern bottles, into which, if you put the rich wine of scientific denial and affirmation, there will be a strange state of affairs.

Mixing beliefs makes mixed results. Remember that. But "If thine eye be single thy whole body shall be full of light."

Scientifically speaking, nothing that is seen with the eye of flesh has reality. It is only our belief about it that we see pictured. The belief that we hold about the reality may be pretty close to the truth of the matter, or it may be very far from the truth, as the picture of yourself in the lake may be a very accurate likeness so far as it goes, or very inaccurate, according to the state of the water, as calm and steadfast or perturbed and ruffled under the summer sunlight.

The carnal intellect is the believing agent. This is not the Self, but the shadow of the Self. The Self is on some mission, and the shadow thereof is carnal intellect. The Self is responsible, and the conscious intellect echoes responsibility.

As it is only an echo, its actions and thoughts are reflective thoughts and actions. When it declares that it is so, it affirms that it cannot think anything of itself. "We are not sufficient to think anything." Then, with that affirmation of the nothingness of mortal consciousness, spiritual judgment awakens. If we keep on with the affirmation, we get out of the reach of physical sensations of evil. We cannot even hear them named. "He that stoppeth his ears and shutteth his eyes from seeing evil, he shall dwell on high."

This demonstrable state of spiritual awakening has not come forth quickly even to the most ardent. "If the righteous scarcely be saved, where shall the ungodly and the sinner appear?"

It is often startling to people who enter upon the study of the Science simply for the sake of the healing argument, to find that there are so many things to know, or that may be known, which seem abstruse, before healing is talked of.

Now, the word naming the study upon which we enter, implies that there are foundation laws and principles upon which the healing practice is based. All practical performances rest upon some principle, which somebody must understand, else the performance stops. The simplest machine is operated by the action of a principle which somebody must understand, else the machine comes to a dead standstill, or runs riot.

The argument for healing will often strike the best mind as so much contradiction of common sense, unless you know why such an argument is scientific. How can you state to a patient that things are not so, if you do not know why they are not so, when his mind agrees with the whole race against your statement? How can you hold your mind firm and steady to the Truth, unless you understand the Truth, and believe firmly and steadfastly in it?

To understand the Principle upon which your practice is based will make you prompt to know what to do with exigencies or strange experiences.

When you are treating a case of insomnia you have to declare that he does not need sleep, because you always tell the patient that he already is just where you desire him to be, and the highest condition the patient wants to be in is to feel that he does not need sleep, but is satisfied with rest; (on the principle of keeping your "eye on the mark of the high calling." as Paul expresses it, or as your drawing teacher would insist upon your keeping your eyes on the point where you want your pencil to stop, when you are making a freehand, straight line.).

When you have treated him wisely he will fall into sweet, refreshing slumber, in order to hasten to the rest you have named, but you may find yourself wakeful and restless as a reactionary experience. What shall you do? Work! "The Lord holdeth mine eyelids waking" — for a purpose. Until you have accomplished that purpose you may not slumber. If any other patient's name occurs to you treat him faithfully. If all your patients are doing well, begin to treat your circumstances, your work as work, say,

*There is nothing in all the world can hinder my words from accomplishing their purpose instantaneously.*

Suddenly you will be certain that your own pride or vanity are stumbling blocks in the way of your accomplishing the highest purposes you have in mind. So you deny the reality and power of vanity and worldliness to keep your words from healing the sicknesses of the people and cleansing them from sinful thoughts. Such characteristics are of mortal unreality. Arise by bold words from such delusions. "Let us take with us words and go unto our God." Perhaps somebody's name and peculiarities may occur to you. Yours may be the kind of mind that believes unconsciously that his or her mind weakens, discourages or hinders; so you set yourself free from such belief in their quality. They may be very innocent of intention to harm you, but your error concerning their peculiar quality needs to be eliminated from your mental atmosphere, by the cleansing law of denial.

This is what the scientist means by work. Never till you have earned the right to sleep will sleep drop from the kindly darkness over your waiting eyelids. "He giveth His beloved to sleep." The early morning is a blessed time — the most blessed time — for you to declare the truth of Life. The day is plastic to you. Write on its still walls your decree that the good and true are victorious already.

Be explicit. Name the special good you would see brought to pass. Declare that it is brought to pass already.

Now if you stand firm the law will lead you up to the sight of the beautiful works done for you by the Truth you have acknowledged so faithfully. By standing firm we mean trusting wholly to the Spirit, ignoring matter's claims.

Trust to the protection of Truth. Be not afraid of anybody's power to harm you. Expect success. All things are promised to the whole-hearted and faithful. Nothing is promised to the half-hearted and faltering.

Stand firmly to your argument when it seems most preposterous. When you look the "paralytic" in the eyes, tell him that he is not helpless and benumbed with your silent thought, though his pitiful face and useless limbs contradict every sentence.

To the truth-loving mind trained to speak of things exactly as the senses tell, it seems like thinking a lie. So you crucify the statement with doubt exactly as the inquisitors tortured Galileo for declaring that the sun does not rise and set, because their own eyes could see it pass from east to west like a grand inspector and judge of earth.

Your senses war with your scientific statement. The conscious mind agrees with the senses' evidence. The real Self, which knows the truth, rests calmly perfect, a steady ray from Most High Wisdom, and lets mortality sublimely alone, except to shine, and ever shine the silent word of Truth into your secret heart.

The Self lets mortality alone; it knows it not. The angels, looking to our identity, knowing us by name, see only the good, the immortal — the rest is blank. We say we see mortally what spiritually is impossible. "Henceforth know we no man after the flesh" — *if we be scientific.*

If you were to hold a smoked glass before the shining noonday sun, it would look pale and murky to you, yet you could truthfully say, "Thou art too bright and glorious for mine eyes to look upon." It would look small and flat like a round plate, yet you could truly say, "Thou art the Light of many worlds, and millions upon millions of living things bask in thy shining, and live by thy warm radiance."

*You take the smoked glass away to prove your words.*

Now the word "Personality", which each of us is in name — a person — is from the word *persona*, a mask, and means *hiding*.

The personal is the bundle of sensations that mortally we are — the sense — and it hides identity, or the Self, which dwells in the heart of Truth and tells only truth, as the smoked glass hides the sun.

The senses state certain things of the Self. You state what opposes them and they vanish into powerlessness before the clear judgment faculty that comes to you.

When the judgment faculty awakens, then the divine Self of you shines and puts all the dark pictures which the senses make, quite away. "Let your light shine."

"The righteous shall not judge after the sight of the eyes." "They shall forget misery, and remember it is as waters that pass away."

"The flesh profiteth nothing." Remove all mortal claims by steadfastly calling them nothing.

Many are staggered by the law that declares we must deny "the world, the flesh and the devil," or the material universe, our sensations, and all evil, and like the disciples of Jesus, go back and walk no more with the Truth. Its rays are too hot for them.

They are sometimes so persistent in holding to the evidences of the senses, that they make the smoked glass — the bundles of sensations, or physical body — blue and acid-looking. They are pale and bloodless while they oppose Truth, fear it, or doubt it. When suddenly its loving light dawns upon them and they cry like Peter, "My Lord and my God," the red blood comes surging through their veins and freshens and beautifies their faces, till they seem fit symbols of the perfect Spirit, with whose word they harmonize.

What queer questions the doubters will ask when you tell them that the material body is nothingness. They will remind you of the immense length of time the material body sometimes takes to disappear, as for instance when it petrifies. "Must not there be reality in that which endures so long?" they ask. Does it make the murky sun anymore of a reality because you remove the smoked glass slowly? These questioners need to be treated to let go a belief in time. It is only in mortal mind that there is time. In Spirit there is only Now. *There is no time.*

They say that the body which we see must go somewhere when it disappears. Ask them where the pale sun went when the smoked glass was removed, or where the shadow of us goes when we leave the surface of the lake. "Dust thou art and unto dust thou shalt return" means, "Nothing wast thou, mortality, and unto nothingness thou shalt return." Jesus said, "Ye are of your father, the devil — a lie from the beginning." Where does the lie go when the truth is told?

Now and then some one whines an objection to saying, "*you have no disease*" because Jesus did not say so. Well, the highest practice toward which we hasten puts our minds where we do not have to say, "You have no disease." We are like Jesus, a tacit rejection of all evil. "Stretch forth thine hand," is a tacit rejection of the apparently palsied hand. "Lazarus, come forth!" is scientific rejection of any death in Lazarus. If we keep our mind steady to Science we shall be a constant destruction to signs of evil. All removal of falsity waits conscious mind's word. "I in the flesh must see God" — I must acknowledge only God.

"Let the waters bring forth abundantly, living creatures." In *Symbology* we are told that the "creatures" of the water signify our conscious affections. The mind acting consciously is the "moving waters." Thus "the invisible things of God are clearly seen by those that are made."

In bringing forth our thoughts for the help of others — the awakening of the best within them — we must deal with their conscious life or conscious way of living and thinking, if we go according to the letter of the law as set down in Mosaic Science.

In our own proceeding to show forth our acquaintance with Truth, we deal thirdly with affirmations respecting ourselves — affirmations proving our conscious and responsible identity. First, we assert the All Being of Good, which announces the true creation. Second, we reject all evidence against that statement. Third, we affirm our relation to the Good.

Now, as bringers forth of thoughts for the awakening of the life and health of our neighbor, we declare that he was not brought forth from the flesh at all, and deny all those sense evidences which the material world imposes, and as thirdly we acknowledged our conscious and responsible identity, so do we meet the patient's third experience of mortality with the word which erases that third error made against him. He is dependent upon our argument to restore him to himself consciously by Truth, the only restorative, the only defense and acquittal from mortality's proceedings. "Do we then make void the law through our faith? God forbid; we establish the law." That law by which he was hastening toward death is no law at all. The only law is the law of life.

After experience with the world of sense, did not the child get to thinking thoughts of good and thoughts of evil, and consciously determine in his heart concerning them? Well, according to his thinking in his heart, so pictured he forth upon his body. "As a man thinketh in his heart so is he." Does it not stand to reason that if thoughts are the causes of disease, we had better be dealing with these causes in curing people than in the diseases themselves; which are only thought pictures?

In reasoning out his conclusions, based upon the evidences of the senses, or the material universe, and after hard study into the so-called laws of the material universe — as climate, food, drink, social relations, etc. — he shares the belief of the race, that somehow or other sin lies as the foundation cause of all sickness, sorrow and misfortune.

It lies heavy on the mind of the race that sin and disease bear a close relation to each other. The man who believes in blind law blindly believes he has broken a law. The miserable savage drawls the weary length of a hundred miles to propitiate his little god of wood and stone for some offense he has committed against it. The religionist writhes with terror lest his disease be the direct consequence of some sin against a wrathful deity.

Outside of perfect Science, sins are never understood as mistakes, errors of judgment, misapprehensions of Good (which they are), but are considered mostly as wicked and willful violations of some known law of God, and therefore their consequences, as sickness and disease leading to death, are expected, and the poor "sufferer," while longing to be free, feels the coils of the law tightening about him, preparing to spring, believing that it is the judgment of God.

All disease is outward evidence of a belief in judgment against sin, on its way to the final punishment of sin, which is death.

Some students of the mind in relation to the body, have insisted that certain sins or mistakes of the mind are sure to show out a certain way, as for instance, they tell us that persistent deceitfulness will make a cancerous condition of the blood; that a certain degree of deceitfulness will bring on diabetes, or a secret slow acidulation by lithic, lactic or uric acids. Constant giving way to anger in youth will bring softening of brain in middle age, we are told; or palpitation of heart, or inefficient lungs; but these conditions are as often the results of being associated with people who have cruel tempers which keep us in constant terror, as of our own tempers. Dreadful accidents, they say, are always occurring in families who constantly give way to fits of temper.

Vicious swellings, like tumors, carbuncles, boils, ulcers, are the results of pent-up jealousy and envy.

Dreadful disappointments are always occurring to ungrateful and unthankful and hypocritical people. "The hypocrite's hope shall perish."

Grasping selfishness strains the functions, the tender stomach and willing fibers fail, and then we wonder why the liver, the stomach or bowels won't work.

Strong will, continually exerted to compel others to do as we would have them, wearies like hard labor, and when it reaches the limit of its power it breaks, and the hands, or knees, or brain, give out in paralysis.

If it is our own intense will or intense pride that has paralyzed us, the case is slow by argument; if it is other people's heavy rod of rebuke laid upon us, the simple words, "You are free," will cause "health to spring forth speedily." Avarice and miserliness will gripe the bowels and warp the nerves. Sensitiveness to praise and blame will swell the heart and spoil the liver.

The word of truth is our freedom. Science teaches the word of Truth. Let us speak it "praying without ceasing."

In treating this girl by strict science, having not the slightest conscious spiritual power, or faith in my own mental efficiency, I was very careful to obey the letter of the law exactly. The best practitioner in the country had told me not to keep on denying the same error blindly as in the dark, but to take one idea at a time and drop it after earnestly denying it once.

There was no difference of opinion in the scientists' teachings as to what mortal errors positively must be denied, and the order of their putting away was clearly put down for me in Scripture, so when this dear one told me, on coming for another treatment, that she was much better and freer from pain after the two treatments I had given her, but that her legs were swollen, her head heavy, and her bowels so uncomfortable from inaction that she could hardly sit still, I knew that there must be some good strong denial of conscious sin sent forth from the mind. She asked me, tremblingly, if her own faults would have anything to do with hindering her getting well. She said she had been thinking a good deal through the night of how her pride and her temper had had their way with her all through her life, and that her life seemed too short to waste it in harboring revenge and ill will. She gave me some family history which showed that the father and grandfather had been violent and cruel-tempered men.

If there is one thing more than another that it seems impossible to make nothingness of, it is the unreasonable anger of a parent against an innocent child or helpless animal. The strong will that will not give right of way to anybody or anything, seems out of the reach of silent denial. The revengeful mind that holds its purposes secret is one to fear greatly, outside of pure Science. So I was confused and dismayed at her description of the family traits which lay back of the rheumatism she had come to be treated for.

It is a good sign for a patient to trust you with his secrets. The Spirit is motherly and forgiving, and draws the broken heart to lean upon it for comfort, if it shines through you.

When she mentioned the characteristics of her family, and her own disposition, I told her how such errors all disappeared under Christian Science treatment, or upon understanding the science, and silently I thought,

"There is no reality in it at all. It is not true that you are all such dreadful sinners."

When she was silent herself I called her name mentally, and said: *Listen to me.*

It took three of four times calling her in the silence to attend to my words with her mind, she was revolving around and round upon her own idea. By and by there was the feeling of the way being direct between myself and her, or as if I were paying all my mental attention to her. Then I talked firmly and definitely as though I were talking aloud:

"You are not suffering any kind of disease or pain at all, rheumatism, or anything else, as the result of your parents' sinfulness or your own sinfulness."

Then I began to feel thick and closed up, as if I could not possibly accomplish anything. The patient seemed locked, or chained, or far off, or some feeling came to me I cannot describe, but which I have since learned is the callousness of the race mind to the accusation of sinfulness. We have been so constantly accused of sinfulness that we do not mind any mental mention of the word.

It is only when something that we might be sincerely sorry for is mentioned, that there is any response to the treatment against sin.

The history of personal, conscious sin begins with selfishness — that supposing that we can have anything to ourselves. "Selfishness is the one sin, and the only sin is selfishness."

The next push of the mind that supposes it can have anything to or for itself, is to envy the possessions of others — to want what others have. And continual envying leads to jealousy, where, the child supposes that somebody has got possession of what belongs to himself. Now that is a foolish supposition, for whatever really belongs to us, that we shall have.

"Lo, my own shall come to me."

Nothing is much more stupid and foolish than jealousy, and it always ends in disease.

Out from jealousy springs malice. There is a maliciousness about jealousy held in the heart that prompts to revenge of some kind, and ends in cruelty if harbored.

The mention of either of these errors will touch the secret consciousness of any mind, and the mention of that one which is the predominating cause of the disease will cause the whole mind to quiver, showing forth upon the body very plainly, if the blow is struck with the wisest mental strength we can bring to the case.

I knew that the idea of sin in general did not appeal to her, by that peculiar feeling that came to me, and I denied that she had inherited any of these characteristics or their consequences.

Did you ever pull up a little plant by the roots to transplant it into better soil. Did you hear the pull as the little roots let go the old soil? There was a strange feeling of something coming up by the roots — I could almost hear the coming, as I said:

"You are not subject to the law of inheritance of sin in pain and disease; you are free from such a law. Spirit is not subject to the sins of the flesh at all; you are spiritual, free, wise and immortal."

"The son shall not bear the iniquity of the father."

As an object is red because it absorbs all the colors of the sunlight, but holds or reflects the red, so is every mind selfish or jealous when it holds or reflects that quality from the race mind surrounding it.

There is but one way to get free from such superincumbent beliefs — denial. So I continued:

"Neither can the whole race mind of error be reflected upon you; the selfishness of the race mind cannot make you selfish, its envy cannot make you envious, its jealousy cannot make you jealous, you know not its malice; its revenge and cruelty have no effect upon you. Mortality cannot stain the child of the Spirit with sin or its consequences."

(The airs around seemed to part, and my patient seemed to me to be like one sitting under the light of a new heaven and breathing in a new atmosphere. But the feeling was only a passing one with me. If it had held steadily with me she would have been healed entirely by that atmosphere.)

"You are not selfish, envious, jealous, malicious, revengeful or cruel, yourself," I said. "Spirit is free from such errors. You are spiritual, free, wise and immortal. You are the child of Spirit; you came down from Heaven, and the Holy Spirit hath washed you with holiness. I do not reflect selfishness upon you; you are not stained by any envy or jealousy in me at all. Malice, revenge and cruelty cannot stay in your presence, child of Holiness.

"You are spiritual, free, wise and immortal. *God is your life.* You cannot be threatened with death, nor fear death, nor yield to death. *God is your health.* You cannot be threatened with disease or sickness, nor fear disease or sickness, nor yield to disease or sickness, ever. *God is your strength.* You cannot be threatened with weakness, nor fear weakness, nor yield to weakness, ever. *God is your peace.* You cannot be threatened with pain or discord, nor yield to pain or discord at all. *God is your peace.* You are not afraid of anybody or anything in all the world. You are perfectly sound and well in every part. You are alive with the life of the Spirit. You are strong with the strength of the Spirit. You trust in God.

"Prove that my words are true by acknowledging to all around you that you are perfectly well. Acknowledge to yourself that you are perfectly well. Acknowledge to me that you are perfectly well and free. Your own words shall testify to the power of the Truth to set free from all the bondage of error. Amen."

Now I was completely lost in the wonderful idea I was conveying to her, and had not noticed any physical effects at all from my thoughts, but when I had finished this argument I opened my eyes and saw that she was crying. "*That will do,*" I said cheerily. The very great practitioners who were telling me of their daily experiences with patients, said that it was a very good sign to stir the unconscious mind of patients till all their former traits and maladies were shown up, by mental argument.

They named many physical symptoms as most excellent outward pictures of mental changes for the better.

I believed everything the successful healers told me. I obeyed all their directions. As I did not claim to know anything about the laws of the Spirit of Truth myself, I had to listen to those who did know, and who proved that they knew by their words. "If I do not know the works of my Father, believe me not." They were all beautiful workers and they spent much time denying the history error. Today the "advanced thinkers" may thank them for their faithful labors.

"My words shall not return unto me void; they shall accomplish that whereunto they are sent." At night I mentally gave the same argument all over again.

Thus did I meet the third error of mortality concerning the divine child of God with the statement of Truth that would make it null and void. Thus were her sins to be washed away by the blood of Christ, and her iniquities remembered no more against her forever.

"In those days and in that time," saith the Lord, "the iniquity of Israel shall be sought for and there shall be none, and the sins of Judah, and they shall not be found."

"If any man will come after me, let him deny himself."

"There is none good but one — that is, God."

There is only God.

Thus, there is only Good.

# LESSON TEN

## Faithfulness to Principle of Healing

Of course the student of Spiritual Life understands that in reality there are no "works" to be accomplished. It is an axiom that *It is finished*. It is an inspiration to realize in the classroom that all so-called healing is but the opening of our judgment to see that what God made is *very good*, and that all that was or is or shall be made is God-made.

Then when we go out of the classroom after a glowing and inspiring lesson on Christian Science Healing, we feel as if we could annihilate a tumor by the mere breath of negation, or dispose of neuralgia by a slight nod of disapproval; but sometimes the tumor and neuralgia seem not so readily obedient to our denials, and the real test of our genuineness of feeling comes by their seemingly refusing to go at our bidding.

What we do when we do not seem to accomplish anything is a better test of our powers than what we do when all things are readily managed. It is the test of our courage and faith.

If the child with diphtheria does not respond after our faithful denial of the reality of such condition, very likely our thought may fly to some "excellent remedy" we have used very successfully in the past.

As the science does not seem to work in this case, we feel as if we verily must bestir ourselves to do something "sensible," instead of sitting there whispering words, which, though they may be efficient enough in some cases, are certainly not working well this time.

We do feel so certain that the remedy would set the child free at once! Hot water, cold water, alcohol, herb tea, or whatever was our favorite healing fetish — shall we not use it?

But if ever we have caught sight of the righteousness of trust in God only, for health, then our mind has lost its faith in materiality, and remedies administered by us now will not have the effect they used to have, because they are no longer vested with the former degree of faith.

The remedies depended entirely upon our faith in them, combined with the faith others also had had in them, but now they are void of all our former alliance and they really will not work with the patient if we administer them. So we may just as well give up hoping anything from alcohol, teas, or hot water, for this turning to them is not confident faith in them, but only hope from them.

What shall we do? Pray. Turn all our thoughts away from the patient and pour them out upon the bosom of the Spirit. We must not beg and plead for a child's restoration. Begging and pleading are not scientific. Our baby does not have to cry and scream for us to give it its breakfast; its little face upturned with expectancy is all sufficient. We are as an infant on the bosom of the Infinite Mother God. Say: "Wilt thou, blessed Mother, present this little one now before us all perfectly sound and well? I thank Thee that Thou didst make her perfect from the beginning, that she is perfect now, and evermore shall show forth as Thou madest her.

"I leave her with Thee in perfect trust that Thou hast heard my prayer and hast served her to perfect health in our sight. Amen."

Speak the lines of this triangle which marks the perfect prayer, over and over till every statement is an absolute reality to you. Then turn to the little one and tell her over and over that there is nothing to fear for the Mother God, folds her round with safety. Tell her she rests in sweet, wholesome, happy health.

Sometimes you may ask another practitioner to treat the case while you pray to God in the way just now described. An ambitious, coarse or deceitful mind should not be allowed to treat your child; neither should a silly or stupid one. After a while you will become very quick to detect the right kind of a practitioner for a particular case.

The spiritually awakened mind is safe for every kind of case. Education in the ways of the world counts for nothing in the treatment of a sick person. One who knows nothing whatever of bones may cure a carious one, which the one who could name and locate every bone would be powerless to relieve. Spirit is the only healing power.

Sometimes all the Christian Scientists you know should be asked to pray for the case that baffles your treatment. Especially should you ask such alliance if there is a lurking desire to have the credit of curing the patient yourself. Pride is a bad ingredient of the mind in the healing practice. It is not nearly so mischievous in the classroom as in the sick room. When there is this characteristic it will be best to arrange it so that nobody shall know who cured the case at all — or rather, whose word prevailed to bring forth the desired health.

Sometimes it takes the combined faith of many to save a life to the world. Once when the Master of Science was talking so entrancingly of health that as many as heard him were cured of their sickness, a palsied man had faith that if he could get near him he also would be healed, but though he got within reach of the great Healer's voice, it was not until his friends had broken open the roof and let him down into the Healer's very presence that his palsy departed. It took the combined faith and active cooperation of all the friends of the palsied man. Let this be to you a lesson when you do so want to "carry the case yourself."

Every day you will show forth new knowledge of the Science of healing if you use the rules faithfully. It is the perpetual creative power of the word of Truth.

He who hath led me to this way,

Still on the way will show;

He who hath taught me of this way,

Still more will make me know.

You will often spring from the regular rule into sudden ideas that the use of the regular rule has taught. For instance, suppose you are treating your son against the appetite for intoxicating drinks, which threatens to hurry him to death or a drunkard's name and shame. When you declare against the effect of the deceptions of his companions, the name of some particular one comes into your mind, or the face of one suddenly appears to your mental vision. You had never thought of this inferior or indolent character as having the slightest influence over your boy's mind, but nevertheless he is miasma to your boy's mental quality (in the mortal mind where they dwell), and you must stop and break off the influence by denying that this one (calling his or her name) can have any power with the free, wise, spiritual Self of your boy.

Often the seemingly boldest and bravest characters are swerved from rectitude by the subtle influence of people who could hardly believe would have the slightest hold on them. Whoever shows such yielding discloses how carnal are his thoughts and how little Science he can command. The truly scientific mind is never affected by any personality. It is as unreal to him as the snakes and toads of his neighbor's delirium.

A noted mesmerist told a Christian Scientist that he could never affect a true Christian with his mesmeric powers, whether he approached him off his guard or when conscious of his attempts. "There seems to be a shield about them that baffles and defies me," he said. Being influenced and affected, or not being influenced and affected by other people's mentality, is a rich test of our Christianity.

There is often a puzzling of young students' thoughts over prayer and the desires of the heart. They notice that their teachers tell them in one breath that in Science all things may be theirs, and to desire anything at all is selfishness.

To the awakened mind there is no discrepancy in the statements. All things are yours because all things are God's. To think of them as yours separate from God would be a species of selfishness appalling to imagine. Prayer for your own to come to you, really means putting yourself in the way of seeing your own by harmony with God. When anything is believed by you to be wrong, why then you are simply believing you can get out of harmony with the Good. So you speak to the Good till you are in harmony of mind, and soon harmony of external conditions will come about you.

When the clouds are heavy and drear outside, the people have been doubting the goodness of God, or doubting that there is any God at all. When there is a sunburst of warm living faith in the goodness of God and His folding presence, then the sun will shine out of doors.

So with your prayers. You get into joyous harmony with the Good by speaking much to the Good, the Father-Mother Presence, and suddenly greater blessings than you have been desiring come to you.

All that Nature made thine own,

Floating in air or pent in stone,

Doth rise the hills and swim the sea,

And like fair shadow fall on thee.

You cut down all thoughts that dispute your harmony with The Good by saying: "I do not doubt that I am safely folded within the everlasting arms of God. I do not admit that I can be homesick, or restless, or unhappy. I deny that there is any evil thing at all between me and Thee, Oh! Eternal Goodness." You keep saying this over and over till you feel as if you could decree that what you desire shall now be made manifest. Do not be surprised if your longing to have the favor in the way you first desired it is quite gone and your heart begins to decree something quite different. Then if you keep on with this scientific mode of praying by denial and affirmation, do not be surprised if your desire changes its name again. Scientific thoughts awaken right judgment to become manifest. Finally you settle down to a knowledge of just what you do want, and then you understand that God hears and answers all the prayers of His children. Also, you understand that all is Yours and nothing at all is yours.

Scientific denials and affirmations will work over the mind so that you do not know your old self. For instance, you have been a miserly mind — that is, you have liked to keep your possessions to yourself, you were not generous. Suddenly you have become poverty-stricken by a failure of some kind. Then you begin to deny the poverty and affirm the supply. By and by you have plenty again, but you are now very generous and wisely benevolent.

If you have been a spendthrift, you become Scientifically prudent. On your way toward these full results of denial and affirmation, you bring up to the surface all your secret faults of character. You had no idea that you were spiteful, but here you are feeling very spiteful. You had no (conscious) idea that you were jealous, but here you are showing considerable of that trait. What brought these characteristics to the surface? Denial and affirmation. "There is nothing covered that shall not be revealed, and hid that shall not be known." Denials are a soluble efficiency, cleansing the mind step-by-step, fault-by-fault. There is no plastering over or hiding our faults after we become Christian Scientists. We are known and read of all men.

We must deal scientifically with our faults when they come to the surface, and we must deal scientifically with our neighbor's faults when they are exposed. "If thou hast heard a matter, let it die with thee." What well of oblivion, what sands of nowhere, so safe as the Scientist's denials?

Most people of the world have errors (delusions) lying secretly folded within the recesses of the mind. Some have had a past so filled with errors that their faces are sodden with discouragement. The more depraved they were, the more hungry for the bread of heaven are they, and thirsty for the wells of righteousness. They have burned to Vesuvian ashes with the fires of their passions. Once we would have chased them with scorn and contumely, with jails and gibbets; but now "show I unto you a more excellent way."

Suppose you have been saying that evil is unreality, and wickedness a delusion, and suddenly you are faced up by seeing some darling child unjustly beaten, or an innocent man wronged by his powerful neighbor. The first thought you have, very likely, is intense indignation, not only at the deeds done, but at the scientific denials, which sound like mockery in the face of such appearances.

Your old way of thinking asserts itself. Your old states of mind are uppermost. Either you used to wring your hands in despair, or fly to take vengeance upon seeing such performances. Now indignation is a sign of power within you to set matters right. Indignation is an excellent servant, but a bad master.

"All misery is faculty misdirected, energy that hath not yet found its way."

If you let the power hide slowly by impotent despair, or disappear by quick revenge, forgetting that, "Vengeance is mine, I will repay saith the Lord," why, you have not directed your faculty aright; not given right way to your energy.

Christian Science has brought the right way to our knowledge. Right in the heat of your intense indignation, send the right word like a cannonball against the error in the mind of the wrongdoer. Say vehemently to him, "No; you cannot harm your neighbor. You are under a law that compels you to do right by him." Every word you speak, and every action you perform is a help, advantage and blessing to him. You must do right. You want to do right.

The man will feel a disinclination to pursue the matter. He will regret that he did the way he did. He will desire to right up matters between them. If you were vehement enough he will make amends in some way.

To one who thinks he has been wronged, say, "No! There has nothing hurt you. No one has wronged you. Every word or action that comes to you is a help, advantage and blessing to you. Look up and rejoice. God is your defense."

He will rouse from his depression and say that an idea has come to him which he thinks he will carry out. He says he believes that, after all, this is the best thing that ever happened to him. From that time he is a success. You cleared his mind of its whole stock of resentment, which had been a latent beclouding characteristic of it, and he is clear to know his own powers and faculties now.

What an excellent exchange of states of mind the scientific practitioner compels. "Let the earth bring forth." Let all that is within thee come forth for a perfect purpose. Let all that is within thee praise His holy name.

How different is the operation of Truth from error. While we dream in error we verily believe that rivers and earthquakes and cyclones and disease have power over our happiness and comfort, but after we know Truth, we know that "these things have no power to hurt."

We learn the changing power of a word. When we hear of great accidents or terrible "dispensations of Providence," by way of earthquake or famine, we say, these things are ended. They are finished. They shall not be upon the earth. We know that every word of Truth we speak is the power of God and will bring "peace on earth, good will to men."

"We crystal sit a new world like our thought." That is, we bring to our view the good world in which we really dwell. We have been seeming to dwell in quite another world. We have imagined things and then seen them. It is not till we think exact Truth that we see the true world.

Guard well your thoughts. Thoughts are things. Thing is a form of think, according to language. They are the same word at the root. "Things are objective thoughts." That is, we see as objects our own thoughts. If we think the thoughts of God we see delightful things.

We think in exact order when we think truly. We begin by stating what we know to be true, and then we reason aright from that foundation premise.

This has the appearance of evolving the mind from the night of ignorance, lighted only by the evidences of the senses, to the day of understanding, lighted by pure Reason. It really is the making manifest of the true Self with its perfect way of thinking.

We deal at the fourth stage of our progress with the necessity for making for ourselves a definite foothold, or ground of faith for the bringing forth of the perfect fruitage of the doctrine. The perfect fruitage of doctrine is: thoughts capable of healing from sickness, saving from sin and waking to righteousness.

First we make the statement of Principle, or as we sometimes say, Statement of Being, giving all place and all power and all intelligence to Good only, which announces true creation with absolute precedence. Secondly, we reject all evidence against the absolute Truth of that seminal principle from its every standpoint. Thirdly, we assert our relation to the Principle, Good, as being of Its creation only. Fourthly, we take our firm stand upon the determination to hold to this statement and work out our problem of life from its basis and line of argument.

On our way to the revelation of our Divine Self, or the intuitive faculty common to all mankind, we come to what is called the trial of faith. The trial of faith is simply the test of our sincerity of willingness to let the Divine Presence take the entire responsibility of our life.

It verily seems that we are asked by the Christ-Presence, the God-Presence, the Father-Presence, the Mother-Love, if we will cast all our care upon It. Many can trust the Divine Presence to heal them of sickness, many can trust the Divine Presence to save them from poverty. Many can trust It to save them from accidents. Many feel reclaimed from sin by the power of the Presence, but hardly any in the world demonstrate that they believe in Its power and willingness to save from all evil.

In laying hold upon this Presence to save us absolutely, we sometimes have to make a strenuous effort of the will to wrench ourselves away from dependence upon other substance than Spirit.

The final decision is the establishing of character, or a *firmament*, as the symbolic story reads.

On the way of error we drifted hither and thither in ways of thinking, for the most part, but upon some things we fixed our mind as true and certain. Those ideas which we were confident of, helped to make our character quality, and built our bodily organs. If we were very fixed and definite in error, some of those organs are called diseased.

Every bodily organ is the translation into a visibility of a fixed way of thinking. Every organ diseased is a fixed error proceeding toward the last result of error, which is death.

Now my patient has a diseased state of the blood and nerves (according to mortal appearance). Therefore, something is fixing an error into her mind that is spoiling her gradually. She is a young girl, but if she keeps on with this erroneous way of thinking she will sometime have bones and muscles well attesting to the fixidity of mind into error.

All patients have been making their calculations about life from the standpoint that they were brought forth according to the laws of flesh into a material universe, taught by its school masters, the senses, and are now according to mortal law hastening toward death.

To this fixed erroneous conclusion of mortality concerning the way of life, you bring the Truth of life. You declare to him, by the denial of conscious and unconscious sin, that the child of Good was never the doer of evil. This statement strikes his guilty conscious and unconscious certainty that his errors or sins in solving his problem of life are to be met by some dreadful judgment. All disease is outward picturing of belief in judgment against sin.

As when a great storm drives over the earth, washing away its landmarks, devastating its growths, muddying, confusing, disturbing all things, but filling this land full of refreshment; as when an alkali is dropped into an acid and a stir and fermentation ensue, but the third property is more serviceable — so will your strongest word stir and astonish your patient.

The strongest error the patient holds against himself is that a child of Good can be a doer of evil.

I have told my patient that she is not guilty of the six sins said to be the conscious inheritance of mortality. This true word she receives in astonishment. The mental state is soon exhibited in a bodily condition.

It shows itself externally as general sickness. She is hot and feverish, in pain all over, and complains of suffering much since I saw her yesterday. All the Christian Scientists had told me that it was a very good sign to stir a patient's unconscious mind sufficiently to show forth bodily in this fashion. Good practical scientists hold such cases with a firm, quiet assurance of mastery.

There is a practice of quieting people down temporarily, by treating them soothingly against pain and sickness, without going back to the causes of pain and sickness in beliefs of sin. But strict Christian Science treatment accomplishes a three-fold cure wherever it is genuinely administered, viz., bodily health, moral reformation, quickened intelligence.

All healing short of this is but partial, and such as the people have had for ages. "Why is the health of the daughter of my people but slightly recovered?" wails Isaiah. Simply because, the flesh alone is considered in the practice of healing. "Thy sins be forgiven thee," is true healing.

I really ought not to fear when this patient of mine complains and shows such signs of general physical misery, because it is *prima facie* evidence that the peculiar error of her mind which showed forth as rheumatism, is hit a hard blow. I have struck the key note to her spiritual nature and physical body, or mortal mind, by the same word. A body resounds when its key note is struck. If the vibration be kept up the body will be pressed beyond its sphere of cohesion and go to pieces. Joshua struck the key note of the walls of Jericho with seven rams' horns blown by seven priests for seven days.

The key note of the iron bridge at Colebrook Dale was struck, and the bridge swayed so violently that the workmen were afraid. The Swiss muleteers tie up the bells of the mules lest the tinkle bring an avalanche down. Chladni mentions an inn-keeper who frequently amused his guests by breaking a drinking glass with the sounding of a certain note. A nightingale is said to kill by the power of his notes. So we cause mortal mind to vibrate when we strike its peculiar error by a word of truth.

It is the unconscious belief in condemnation for guiltiness that I have struck. In Truth, "There is therefore no condemnation." Condemnation is discord.

Why did this girl frighten me by such signs of confusion and disturbance of mind? Because her mental disturbance was a state of fear, which she communicated to me, and because I had always been taught to judge by the senses and not by righteous judgment, or according to true reason. What her body showed forth I feared, but I bore in mind the fourth statement of the rule of health, and denied every word she said with a firm mental No! I repeated the word, rallying more and more steadiness and quiet firmness till I was ready to say to her just the word she needed, which was the fourth statement of the great rule of health. This is the fourth statement of the rule as I gave it to her in the silence.

"Listen to me — you are not disturbed or frightened at all by anything I have said to you. I have not condemned you. Spirit does not condemn you. There is no condemnation. All is peace. Spirit cannot be disturbed or frightened. Spirit has not inherited the consequences of guilty fears or discords or inharmonies of flesh, and Spirit is not disturbed by the fears or discords of the whole mortal race. You are not confused or disturbed by the fears of the people around you, and you are not disturbed by your own fears. You are not affected at all by my fears for I am not frightened or confused by anybody or anything. You are free and fearless; you are steady and peaceful, you are true and steadfast; you are strong and well. Because God is your life, you cannot be threatened with death, nor fear death, nor yield to death at all.

God is your health; you cannot be threatened with disease or sickness ever. God is your strength; you cannot be threatened with weakness, nor feel weakness, nor yield to weakness ever. God is your peace; you cannot be threatened with discord or inharmony of mind or body nor yield to discord or inharmony of mind or body at all."

Your trust is in God.

Peace, peace, peace.

My peace give I unto you.

The peace of God that passeth understanding,

Keep your heart and mind.

"You are ready to acknowledge to all around you that you are well and at peace.

"You are ready to acknowledge to me that you are well and at peace."

I said aloud to her. "That will do." She was quiet and free from pain. She seemed drowsy. I told her to go home and sleep awhile.

I said mentally, "My words shall not return unto me void, they shall accomplish that whereunto they are sent." At night I remembered her and gave her the same treatment absently.

This experience of Truth meeting error is called "Chemicalization." Chemicalization means taking a new base, whether we refer to the process of mind or the changing of organic substance to recombine as new compounds, which our chemists tell of.

It is a most excellent term because it is exactly the same with mind as in the chemist's laboratory, that the new base is what follows the removal or alteration of some necessary ingredient to the old compound.

The peculiar sin which was a necessary ingredient of the old mind is removed or altered, and the patient's mind will never be the same after his special sin is met by the word of absolute truth.

142

Sometimes people are quite ill (in appearance) when we tell them that their mistake, or the so-called sin which has built the lameness or neuralgia, is quite gone.

The unconscious mind refuses to let go its delusion. But it is the nature of mental denial to loose error from the mind, so the patient will have to let go the notion which made his disease, if the practitioner is bold and determined.

Whenever the mind has let go of its enviousness, the rotten bone will be healed.

"Envy is the rottenness of the bones." "Pleasant words are health to the bones."

Whenever you let go your belief that there is death in the world, the paralyzed arm will thrill with life.

You are on a higher mental base when you do not hold the old trait of character you used to have, or get angry so easily as you used to do.

If you drop the old trait willingly and naturally, the body will not act queerly. It will turn from sickness to health at once quite simply and easily. Of course health comes by the word, but the mind is so willing that the body shows forth the step "from death unto life," gently.

You are able to cause other people to step forth as health and goodness by a true word. Tell them that they were not made proud and deceitful, and they will show by their bodies just how closely they hug the habit of deception and pride, or how they love the truth.

The practitioner must hold on and hold out till the patient has quite let go, whether willingly or unwillingly.

The chemist holds patiently by till the acid and alkali have stirred and fermented in the jar, and the new base is formed — the right compound, the serviceable material for his experiments.

The farmer waits with rejoicing for the great rainfall to cease from disturbing his fields, knowing what excellent soil the refreshed earth will be for his seeds.

Joshua cried, "Shout for the city is ours!" when the walls were tumbling.

Shout, for the situation is in your hands when the patient shows signs of yielding by giving a seemingly bad account of his body, which is only the shadow of his mental state.

Everybody seems to be afraid, and in discord and inharmony, when their mind is searched around, and some people show it one way and some another.

Now and then a patient will be shocked into great stillness by the denial of evil traits.

We are told to give the treatment against fear in a rapid and invigorating way when there is a stiffened or paralyzed fashion of receiving the renovating treatments.

If we take it excitedly, by showing fever and general sickness, speak nothingly and gently.

The touch of mind we use in silent teaching, they will catch.

Be very, very coldly quiet to an asthmatic or inflammatory excitement.

There is a way of treating people just simply for bodily sickness, without stirring up the hidden causes in moral character, and doing very good temporary patching up of bodily health. But such slipshod work is not Christian Science healing.

Swedenborg tells us that we can deal with the physical body on a physical plane up to a certain point, after which, if the character be not true and upright, there is no possible health for the body.

To treat simply against disease is a sort of hypnotizing of the senses. To treat for character-cleansing is Christ ministry.

Those, who practice hypnotizing, or what is called mesmerizing, tell us that it is almost impossible to control an intelligent person.

This is an intelligent age, and no cure short of character-cleansing will appeal to the judgment of the people.

If an attack of diphtheria seizes upon a child, some discord or inharmony has impressed its mind with fear. There is enmity between peace and turmoil. Deny discord.

Sometimes a mother's unjust reproof, or a father's sternness is the cause of the diphtheria. Their conscience resented their own words even as they spoke them. Deny inharmony. The child is frightened. We must treat gently and tenderly and soothingly against the fear.

# LESSON
# ELEVEN

## Regulation and Pious Regime

## vs. Healing

"And God said, Let us make man in our image after our likeness, and let them have dominion."

That miraculous healing is done by the workers of Christian Science, is an acknowledged fact. That they do these wonderful cures by a method not taught in the medical colleges is understood by the people at large. That their greatest miracles are wrought upon what the most learned in medical lore have denominated "incurable cases," calls the attention of unprejudiced thinkers to the idea that there must be a way of making sick people well, superior to any way known to or practiced by the M.D.'s.

That extraordinary moral reformations are brought about by the Christian Scientists, is a verified proposition. That they reform drunkards and change vicious dispositions, has been noted as greatly to the credit of the mysterious practice by which the changes are wrought. No strong cups of coffee, or strategy of keeping the rum bottle out of sight (regulation methods) and yet the drinker no longer drinks. No tears, or vengeance, or weak condoning (pious regimen), for ill-temper, and yet loving tenderness has taken its place.

That multitudes of seemingly stupid and inferior people have suddenly sprung into notice as "teachers of men" and intelligent preachers of a powerful doctrine, is the wonder (and disgust) of the unsuccessful plodders along the prescribed lines of Theology, Law, Political Economy, *Materia Medica.*

Why is not the knowledge of how such results are reached a knowledge worthwhile?

Supposing the students of plants, planets, bones and suns, do laugh at the healing, reforming, quickening demonstrations of Christian Scientists, it is certain that they cannot do the works that the Christian Scientists do, and that therefore what the Christian Scientists know is practically more worthwhile than what they know.

When I asked a modest Christian Scientist how he had proceeded to cause an ugly tumor to disappear from a "poor woman" in one "treatment," he answered, "I held with all my might and main, the thought that 'All is Spirit' and in Spirit there are no tumors. As I held this thought I forgot that I had ever tolerated such a false notion in my mind as that a substance called matter existed, with tumors, boils, deformities, etc. to be put away. I do not know how long I held with all my mind to the truth that 'All is Spirit', but when the woman spoke aloud in great excitement that her tumor is going, I seemed to have been for a long time absent from the senses and present with the Spirit — *One with Spirit.*"

I asked a gentle-voiced practitioner of the Christian Science way of healing, how she had compelled a "bed-ridden sufferer" to arise and dress herself within an hour after her first visit.. She replied, "I knew with my whole mind that 'there is but One Will,' and that that Will is against feebleness and suffering. I realized that if there is but One Will, and that Will wills always strength, health, vigor, then any other conditions must be only appearances and not realities. So I declared, 'One Will, One Will,' over and over, till I was myself so lost in that Will, that *I was* that *Will*; then I said aloud, *Get up and dress yourself*; and she obeyed."

I asked a loving-hearted woman how she cured that "long-suffering" case of consumption after such a short acquaintance. She explained, "I learned early in the study of the Science of Life that 'There is but one Life,' exactly as Spinoza and Swedenborg told us.

The words, 'There is but one Life,' had been constantly with me. As that Life is eternal, unbroken, unchangeable, any appearances of cutting off of Life, or checking, or consuming, must be delusion, error.

He who thinks that he can slay a life,

Or he who thinks Life can be slain,

These both do err, for Life is God,

And God cannot be slain.

"With this thought I seemed to look straight into the flowing, ceaseless, streaming life of the woman. This was all I did. She is full of vigorous life now. It seems to flow through her to enliven and refresh other people, too."

I questioned a man who had healed another man of "blindness" in one treatment, as to how he did it. He said, "I had been holding on to one idea for quite a while. It was, 'There is but One Law. One Law — One Law. We are all under that Law. Nothing can escape that Law. The Law is. See, see, hear, hear, live, live, speak Truth, speak Truth. Anything or anybody claiming not to see, hear, live, speak Truth, isn't here at all, as all that is real is under the One Law.' I forgot that there was anybody claiming to be there asking me to heal him. This state of my mind cured him."

I questioned a woman who had been snubbed by the literary society of her town for "rather lacking in mental acumen," as to how she raised that "dying case," with the mind seemingly departed, into smiling intelligence and joyous health. She said, "It had been in my mind continually that there is but One Mind Thinking thoughts; perfect thoughts. 'Thoughts are things.' The things of the One Mind are perfect, because 'God is the One Mind'. Then it was nonsense to think there was anything or thought imperfect. I could not think so. I had never been given power to think so, for God made me perfect. I was One with the perfect Mind thinking perfect things. I forgot the patient. I was lost in gladness of Mind. This word and feeling on my part lightened the face and stirred the blood of the patient."

One who had trouble in her home, said silently, "Spirit is All Peace." Then the home became peaceful. Another said, "Spirit is the Only Healer" and some cataracts fell off. She thought, "Spirit will bring it to pass," and a seemingly dying mother got up and took care of her children. Her favorite text was, "Rest in the Lord and He shall bring it to pass." Her strongest certainty was, "Not by might nor by power, but by My Spirit, saith the Lord."

A theologian said that these people were sacrilegious and anti-Christ, and warned his flock against listening to their teachings. But his "flock" went slyly to the Christian Scientists, were delighted with the idea of Oneness of God, or the Unity of Good, and secretly told him God's Love flowing through him caused him to be good and kind — which "treatment" was so effectual that his little wife's pale face changed to happy pink, because he had praised her.

I met a former skeptic in religious matters (now an ardent Christian Scientist), and asked her what had appealed to her reason in the arguments of this new Science, and she said:

"It is not a new science, my friend; word-healing is as old as man, and that the words must be true to do good healing is a common-sense proposition. I went to studying those words which had accomplished most miracles in the world. They are a correct deduction from the universal conviction in the heart that there is a God — Omnipresent, Omnipotent, Omniscient.

"Every statement made by the Christian Scientists is an almost verbatim quotation from some ancient thinker. I do not believe the Christian Scientists live any more truly by these teachings than did those who formerly proclaimed them. And as for healing the sick, theirs are far below the works accomplished by former healers by formulas. The only credit the Christian Scientists can take to themselves from first to last, is that they have boldly determined to compel the world to listen to these much neglected teachings, and see how and wherein they coincide with the teachings of the Bible writers and Jesus of Nazareth.

"That God is Omnipresent Spirit is ancient teaching sustained. That God is Life Omnipresent, is the 'One Life Universal' of the past doctrines. That Truth is Omnipotent God, Plato repeated from his instructors. The Omnipresence of Spirit precluding the reality of matter, is external reasoning. In the Hindu *Lanka Vetara* we read, 'What seems external exists not at all.' Gautama Buddha said, 'Beware of the delusions of matter.' How do we 'beware of the delusions?' By knowing Truth, of course. Then knowing Truth is freedom from material conditions. As Jesus said, 'Ye shall know the Truth and the Truth shall make you free'.

"The Unity of God as Spirit is old teaching revived. God is Good is an axiom. So, judging the righteous judgment' of Jesus Christ, Good is Spirit Omnipresent. In highest moments of inspiration all the sages of the past said, 'evil is negation — non-entity, and matter is *non est.*'

"That there is no life substance intelligence, in matter; no sensation in matter, no reality in sin, sickness, death, is teaching so old I cannot name the years, for the Eastern Sages tell me, more than seventy thousand.

"Truth is not troubled by matter nor cumbered by body, but is naked, clean, unchangeable. 'Truth is only in eternal bodies which very bodies are Truth.' (This was a saying found on a tablet in the valley of Hebron after the flood.) Plato taught that ideas are the only real thing, and that God is the ruling Principle."

Berkeley affirmed that there is not any other substance than Spirit. Fichte said, 'Outside mind there is no existence.' Plotinus said, 'Matter is neither soul, nor intellect, nor life, nor form, nor reason, nor bound, and cannot merit the appellation of being, but is deservedly called non-entity. Sensation is the faculty or employment of the soul.' The Zohar teaches that the real man is Spirit.

"To cure by saying, 'God looks you quite away' was a former mode of treatment of disease, equivalent to saying, 'I look at you, therefore you are nothing.' For the Supreme feeling in speaking these words must be that there is but One looking, and that is God. At the healing moment of this word, I feel as if I were that One who is looking. This feeling is engendered by the word, and the fruit is a manifestation of health, or morals, or intelligence, in the one meeting my word, or rather where my word sweeps over. 'There is but One Being.' All Truth spoken is the speaking of that One Being, who is Truth. All that is not true is not said, for there is but One Speaker. 'God looks you quite away' is our denial of sickness put another way."

This woman had not been well or happy formerly, but such reasoning had made her both well and happy.

As a young practitioner in the science of healing by the realization of Truth, I saw that I had got to make such statements and hold to them bravely, right in the face of every mortal appearance and every preconceived notion. Every teaching of my youth was opposite to such words. Every friend I had in the world scorned them. Indeed, they scorned me for fellowshipping with them that believed the words.

If the words were true how foolish the world had been to let go its hold of them. How ignorant of them shows the poor world now. "Fools die for want of wisdom." So all the death and sorrow of the world might be swept away if only the world could know that, 'All is Spirit; matter is delusion.'

Feeble and dying with ignorance of the Sea of Omnipotence, from which to drink strength for the day. Fainting for lack of knowledge of the Airs of Omnipresence, from whence to breathe refreshment for each instant. Discouraged, through not knowing of the Sunlight of Omniscience, from whose glory to draw understanding to "be strong to do exploits."

Foolish because with all the teachings and demonstrations of the past, they would not receive. "Ye will not come unto me that ye might have eternal life."

With all the teachings and concerning Omnipresence, Omnipotence and Omniscience, we have still believed in the foolishness, weakness and brokenness of Mind.

"According to thy faith be it unto thee." So our false faith "hath hewed us out broken cisterns," and walled us in "chambers of imagery."

As I meditated in this way, a stern resolve seized upon me. I would be one with many, or one alone, to stand true to the teachings which, when faithfully put into practice, would work such salvation.

I would realize that if I did not work miracles it would be because I had not made myself One with the Principle I had now been taught.

I would never say, "I cannot accept this point;" or, "I do not receive that proposition;" no, I would let each proposition accept me, mold me, use me. Each tried and proved axiom — I myself would be that axiom.

I would never say I could not cure the worst form of sickness. I would not say that anybody could not cure; I would keep the word "failure" off my list, if "for the lightest word I must give account."

I would do the very best I knew at every instant. By doing my best I should be serving the Best, and the Best would take care of me. Every prompting I would heed as a message from the Spirit. For there is but One Mind thinking thoughts.

Soon I learned to have surprise at one who described vividly the former diseases of a fellow man, for the law reads, "They shall forget misery as waters that pass away." It was given to me to see that some practitioners brought back upon their well friends their former maladies, by remembering them for them. "If thou hast heard a matter, let it die with thee."

After mentally resolving to stand, faithful to the proposition, "Spirit is All," because Reason teaches it, and revelation or demonstration sustains it, I could understand what all these practitioners whose words I have quoted, meant, when they insisted that I must know everything as a sign of success in "treatment of cases."

I did not like what they called "treating cases," very well, but I was told that only by so doing, faithfully giving forth my silent arguments, day after day (what Paul called "holding fast the form of sound words"), could I enter into the ability to do instantaneous spiritual healing — demonstrate Redemption.

If I should be suddenly filled with fear, they said I must regard it as a sign that my "patient" was chemicalizing and must be treated to be steady to the truth I had told. I must harness every sign to the chariot wheels of success. Call fear by name and tell it to go to the ends of the universe to bring me fearlessness. The other side of fear is fearlessness. It is a servant, not a master. Whatever we bid it do, that it will do. It will turn like a veering wind at our command, and from bearing down against us, will blow our white sails into the port we long for — success.

If all our silent words seem to go like shining arrows against a hard wall of opposition in the patient's mind, regard it as a sign that we must drop "the form of sound words," or the "regular argument," and meet that particular case by its own argument, as, you cannot present a wall of error so hard, or so thick, or so impenetrable, but that the word of Truth can shatter it all to pieces, then go on with the regular reasoning.

If all our words seem to fall into a vacuum and be lost in nothingness, this also is its own signal. Drop all the reasoning and say, "There is nothing wrong here. There is nothing at all wrong — nothing at all. All is well." Then affirm perfect health and strength as manifest now.

If there are signs of death by the school teachings, regard them as signs of Life by the Spirit's teachings.

Say silently to what you formerly called signs of death, "old conditions are dead, quite dead. You are awake and alive to the truth." Speak these words fervently many times over. Speak them till you are as lost in them as those beautiful workers I have just told you about. Paul says, "We must be dead to sin."

Metaphysicians call it chemicalization when one who has been treated mentally shows signs of confusion and discord, either of mind or body. He fights the Truth. But if those who are speaking Truth mentally will hold faithfully to their words, they will see the Truth prevail. The man who has Truth and Right on his side, can stand calm and serene amid the clash of heated oppositions.

All Truth is calm, refuge and rock and tower;

The more of Truth the more of calm;

Its calmness is its power.

Do not doubt that the Truth will prevail. Truth is omnipotent — irresistible.

For Right is Right, as God is Good,

And Right the day will win;

To doubt would be disloyalty,

To falter would be sin.

Truth is Intelligence and Justice. We cannot pretend to trust Truth, and fear failure. "God is not mocked." To learn to have the conviction that Truth will show through the sorrow and pain of the world, great joy and peace, is that "Secret of the Lord," after which the devout in all ages have yearned.

It is astonishing to us to meet the unwillingness of the people to receive the pure reasoning of metaphysics. They are told that Spirit is the Only Substance. They had other aims in life; other than spiritual things from which they hoped to get satisfaction. How can they turn from them to what is so invisible to their senses? Thus they are weighted by their material thoughts and say they cannot take the leap into, "All is Spirit." There is a continual discord between the Truth that calls and the error that holds. While this state of mind obtains they have sickness, pain, misfortune, as outpicturings of discord of mind.

Some have for a long while opposed Bible teachings, and do not like to find how many Bible writers understood pure science in certain moments. Some do not like spiritual interpretations of Bible history. They have so long read them carnally.

Some do not want to be told that all who know Truth must preach it. "Woe is me if I preach not the gospel." Some find that their "Sphere" is their home. Awakened judgment tells them so. They had wanted to do public work. Some have been proud of their material knowledge, and its foolishness is very apparent in their attempts to heal the sick, reform sinners and raise the dead. "Not the wisdom of this world, nor the princes of this world."

Doubts are nipping frosts to some people. Every seeming failure discourages them. They are in a constant state of chemicalization, till, finally, some grand day, they "surrender heart and will and reason," to Truth.

Every outshowing of what is undesirable is the fruit of opposition to Truth. Harmony with Truth is Harmony of environments.

"With all thy getting get understanding" — of Spirit. "Seek ye first the Kingdom of Spirit, and all these things shall be added unto you." "I have said that I would observe Thy words."

The skilled teacher sees through the student's confusion the good worker coming, and the skilled practitioner sees through chemicalization the new man arising — like the refreshed earth after the driving storm, like the third property after acid and alkali have mingled to decompose old conditions and show forth the serviceable base.

Such faith is always rewarded by clear seeing. After the confusion of mind that shows as fever, comes the stillness of truth prevailed. After the shock of mind at having its special error named, sets in the health current.

We tell every man, woman and child, that it is an error to call them sinners. God made them "Very Good." They must show this Truth forth.

It is very good news — gospel tidings — which gives Truth for error. This is the gospel of forgiveness — giving for mistakes, Truth.

"Let us make man in our image, after our likeness; and let them have dominion."

"All sudden changes or severe attacks are signals that a Truth has been told that struck a special error. Even if there is no (what is called) Christian Science teaching going on, yet all sickness is sign of a Truth spoken, not yet accepted.

The able workers whom I interviewed had held to some straight lines of reasoning for many days before they received their Supreme statement so perfectly that they were themselves IT.

They carefully went over line upon line and precept upon precept of their usual formulas for healing. From among them all, put with the Scripture teachings, I found that after severe chemicalization, people are often found weak and nerveless. They are like as if they had carried a heavy burden a long way, and after laying it down, feel relieved, but exhausted.

Now weakness, weariness, exhaustion, languor show a state of mind just ready to be worked up and over by Absolute Truth. It is the insipid base of the mental laboratory.

To be sure, weakness is to be denied, and exhaustion is no evidence of the dominant character, so far as sense perception can judge; but, nevertheless, it is the stage where the bold, strong truth teller can "make" or cause to stand forth, the child of dominion.

What are the signs of dominant character? Intelligence, Strength, Energy, Boldness, Health, Vigor, Endurance. These are the birthright of the child of God. Showing the opposite of these is showing forth ignorance of our birthright.

Showing weakness or feebleness is showing that one has believed that so-called nature has dominion over him instead of he over nature. He has believed that nature would punish or reward him for eating, drinking, sleeping, etc., when the fact is, he is governor of nature.

Treat such with the fifth statement of the Scientific rule of Health.

"We must have a reason for the hope that is in us." Anybody under the ministration of our word must have the right word given him. "A right word, how good it is." And each of us can speak the right word to match every seemingly false state — "speak it with judgment, not blind repetition as the heathen."

Just as good cures have been wrought by the faithful "keepers of the law," or observers of the right word, as by those who realize the Truth so vividly; though their work is not always so quickly manifest.

A single point in itself worthy of separate argument, held faithfully, runs the river of peace down through us to bless all unto whom we minister. "I will extend peace like a river, and glory like a flowing stream."

Reject the discouragement of foolishness. There's a reason for pronouncing it an unreality. Reject the feebleness of ignorance. There's a reason for calling it delusion.

Announce the vigor and judgment of the child of God. There's a reason for calling him "very good."

Filled with such thoughts as this lesson has considered, I went boldly to the boarding place of the young girl, to whom I had given four faithful reasonings.

She sent for me, as being herself "too feeble to come out" (the messenger said). At first I was beaten down by the sight of her. "My heart fainted within me." The fact was, I had been school-taught so exactly in accordance with her appearance, that I fell right in with it as the reality, in spite of the new reasonings which had quickened my heart "to hope in the Good."

She did look feeble sure enough. She was wan and pale; she hardly breathed; she spoke fretfully; she certainly seemed to be blaming me for her condition. She began to rehearse how miserable she had been the past four days; dreaded more misery like it; feared Christian Science treatment wouldn't work with her, though it might do for others.

"Irritability is a good sign," said a successful practitioner. "Meet it by the right word. Deny foolishness and ignorance. Wise, capable people never get irritated. Affirm strength, judgment, vigor. Give a reason mentally for strength, judgment, vigor, as the birthright of the child of God."

I remembered her words. I also remembered my classroom teacher's words urging us to deny every evil thing. "It is nothing at all," she had said; "Only Health is Reality." So I said with a loving firmness of mental tone, "No." The word gave me more firmness, and I spoke it silently with gathering courage. It almost seemed as if I held her close to me, I spoke so strongly and kindly, like a reassuring mother. "There have been many people cured by our just saying 'No' when they tell us of their ailments," said a successful little worker.

Why shouldn't my denial of her saying cure this girl? I thought. Yet when she stopped talking I did not feel certain in any sense of the word, that she was well and strong and vigorous. So I proceeded to give her a regular argument, calculated to encourage and strengthen her mind. The words would have been absurd if it had not been for the law of the efficiency of silent thoughts in bringing about bodily cures.

How glad I was that I knew exactly what to say to one who claimed to be exhausted and feeble and made it seem so real to me. I had not then been able to make the words, "All is Spirit," or "All is mind," or "All is Will," or "All is God," do any healing for my patients. I had to speak word after word in orderly argument to make anything seem reasonable at all to me, while what seemed to be a sufferer sat or lay waiting for me to cure her.

All the courage gained while absent from the sights and shows of matter, cozened when the claim of suffering appeared.

Gautama Buddha once wrote, "He who knows the order of the letters, those which are before and those which are after, he is the sage."

I knew the "letter of the law" which followed on after the common result of effectually telling a patient that his special sin is really nothingness, and that he is not under condemnation.

"You are not feeble and tired," I said mentally. "You are not suffering from a heredity of foolishness and ignorance. I deny that you are under the law of heredity. There is no such law." (Do we then make void the law through our faith? God forbid. We establish the law. That which has been called law is no law at all; therefore, peace and rest are our portion.)

"You are not under the race burden of foolishness, nor its shadow of ignorance. You are free from race burdens. None of these things move you. I deny the delusion of a race law.

"You do not suffer from contact with the foolishness and ignorance of the people around you. They cannot weight you with foolishness, nor darken you with ignorance. I deny the claim of association. I deny contagion, mental or physical. I deny environment. I deny restrictions and limitations. I declare you free born and strong in the love of God.

"You are not burdened by your own foolishness, nor darkened by your own ignorance. I deny the mortal law of cause and effect. God is your Cause, and Love and Strength are your everlasting right.

"I cannot hold you in weakness by my foolishness, nor keep you faint by my ignorance. I am Life and Love to you; I am strength and health to you.

We are One in God.

We are One in Love.

"God is your Life, you cannot be threatened by death, nor fear death, nor yield to death. God is your everlasting Life. God is your Health, you cannot be threatened with sickness or disease, nor yield to them ever. God is your everlasting Health.

"God is your Strength, you cannot be threatened with weakness, nor fear weakness, nor yield to weakness, ever. God is your everlasting Strength. God is your Peace, you cannot be threatened with discord or inharmony of mind or body, nor fear discord or inharmony of mind or body, nor yield to them, ever. God is your everlasting Peace.

You are alive with the Life of the Spirit.

You are strong with the strength of the Spirit.

You are bold and vigorous and hardy and energetic and tough and enduring.

You are strong and free and well.

You are acknowledging to all around you that you are strong and free and well.

You acknowledge to me that you are strong and free and well.

God is Life, God is Truth, God is Love.

After these words, spoken in the silence very earnestly, I waited a minute or so, shaken by the Spirit of them into a new state of mind.

By and by I opened my eyes and found that she was sitting upright looking at her hands, which she showed me were turning pink, and felt very warm. Her cheeks had a pretty color, and she said she felt a hot glow all through.

I told her to come to me the next day, and silently I decreed, "My words shall accomplish that whereunto I have sent them."

"Thou shalt decree a thing and it shall be established unto thee, and the light shall shine upon all thy ways."

All the way to my room I kept whispering the words, "Omnipotent Love, — Omnipotent Love." When I got there I found a lady waiting for me who desired treatment for a peculiar malady. As we sat in the silence I could not find any words to say at all. Yet she came the next day to tell me that she was perfectly cured by that one "treatment." Thus was fulfilled in me the promise, "He that is faithful over a few things, I will make him ruler over many."

And such reasonings are the metaphysical practice which is calling the astonished attention of the nineteenth century. "This is the stone which the builders rejected, that has become the head of the corner."

# LESSON
# TWELVE

## Teaching and Ministry

The student of Spiritual Law, when he realizes the wonderful potency of silent thought, gets to resting in his inaudible ideas, and sometimes when a patient really would get manifestly well more quickly if audibly spoken to, the student does not show wisdom enough to tell him the little points which would help him so much.

There really are people who are thirsty and hungry for the true doctrine, line upon line and precept upon precept.

Many who could speak wisely and beautifully and help to convert to sound faith their patients, leave them waiting for perfect healing till some other practitioner, more gracious and just, tells them what they have so unconsciously longed to know.

When a "dyspeptic" tells you she is hungry, that is a signal thrown out for you to tell her she can eat anything and everything she wants.

When a "cripple" tells you he feels an impulse to use his limbs, tell him to do so at once.

When a "long-time invalid" turns her mind away from her own body length of time enough to talk of some other theme till she is honestly interested in it, she is ready to get up and go to work.

True harmony with the Principle stated in pure Metaphysics, will express itself through you either by audible word or silent thought in exactly the right fashion.

True harmony is discovered by steady reasoning. Steady reasoning compels the mind to love to see Truth expressed better than any other thing. To carry the gospel is the sole ambition of the genuine lover of Truth.

When, in carrying on his ministry of the Word, his days are charged with unwonted tasks and his sights with unexpected cares, the lover of Truth does not flinch, and he knows no weariness or resentment. "they shall run and not be weary; they shall walk and not faint."

He knows himself as the servant of the King, and he does not fear but that the King he serves will faithfully reward him.

To be so one with the Principle he professes that his word is performed exactly as he decrees, is the delightful reward of the student and practitioner of Divine Principle.

Sometimes the reasoning which discovers the harmony of the Mind of man with the Mind that is God, is by unvoiced speech, and sometimes by definitely spoken, audible words. To be honestly determined to do the best and wisest way will keep the student from extremes, from settling back into a habit of inward meditation on the one hand, or from talking too much on the other.

There is nothing sincere workers so desire as to go on in the science," that is, to understand it more and more. That is well. "With all thy getting get understanding." This righteous desire often seems to have a shadow running subtly along by its side. The shadow is the thought that we must understand more of the Principle before we can demonstrate it. This is not true. We must demonstrate it in order to understand it. By demonstration is meant faithful declaration of the law at all times and under all circumstances.

"Do the will to prove the doctrine."

The student who listens to any plausible suggestion will soon receive himself into a theorist, with vague postulated forever slipping between the fingers of hope and never satisfying with substantial good.

The highest truth has its opposite statement, and the most righteous intention has its contradiction.

The opposite statement and the contradiction are pure nothingness. Heed them not.

Rehoboam was the enlarger of the people by substantial right, but by listening to error he enlarged his enemies instead of his friends.

We are efficient understanding in Truth, but in error we wait and hope for efficient understanding.

We must use and use every word of Truth we hear and think, sending it forth over the waiting people near and far, for the declared purpose of showing them forth well and sound and strong and joyous.

The word of Truth is the Spirit that can preach the gospel, heal the sick, cast out demons, raise the dead.

The highest theory of music is cold and elusive, unless by practice, practice, practice of the wonderful combinations we wake symphony, sonata, and requiem to charm the heart to forgetfulness of discord. The living hold on harmony is what practice brings.

"*Diligence passe sens.*"[3] The glowing understanding of the Health, Life, Peace, Strength, that surround us, is the, gathering thereof within ourselves as "threads are closed in a weaver's shuttle" to warm and comfort and brace and heal the world. The whole of understanding is the power of ministry. The more we minister, the brighter our understanding.

The more actual figuring a mathematician practices, the better he understands mathematical principles. Laws and principles are for the battle ground of daily experiences.

All the advantages which Truth brings, She brings because of our loyal service.

More than thou canst give to truth

Will she on thee confer,

If thou wilt all thy youth

And all thy strength give her.

Take everything that looks or sounds undesirable and squarely meet it with the Omnipotent word of Love. Such use will enlarge and toughen the muscles of mind till there is nothing of error that will or can seem to have any power in it.

---

[3] "Diligence overcomes feeling." (French)

Omnipotence knows no resistance. You are Omnipotence (as Truth), therefore you know no resistance.

All the ways of error soon lie as open pages of delusion and powerlessness before the lovely speaker of Truth, whose sole motive is to make Good visible.

The ways of mortal mind are open to the spiritually minded, and every word of denial is a Damascus blade to cut down its claims.

We never hear the spiritually-minded tell that people with false ideas give them false judgments, materially-minded people weight them down and weary them, sordid people smother them, sensual people give them nausea, deceitful people irritate them, etc. No. They tell of the everlasting protection of the Spirit; "He will give His angels charge over them to keep them." They speak joyously of the defense of the Spirit: "There shall no ill come nigh thy dwelling."

They sing of their freedom and lightsomeness of heart: "The Lord God is thy sun and shield."

They do not believe in poverty: "Thou shalt have plenty of silver."

They do not fear the evil speech or foolish words of friends or foes, silent or audible: "Thou shalt be hid from the scourge of the tongue."

They are not afraid to read any book they please. They do not believe that any mental influence can darken or shake them. "None of these things move me." They know how to negative the mental quality of writers whose thoughts would by mortal claim discourage or dishearten the habit of receptivity to error believed to be the characteristic of patients.

They detect the spiritualizing and awakening effects of certain books, as able to turn the mind from sordidness and depression to peace and strength.

They know when to ward off the sarcastic flashes of book writers, and the merciless witticisms which mortal sense declares cut off the head of peace and hope.

They declare scientifically against the intellectually taught, who by matching intellect with intellect claim to tire and suffocate the sick.

They do not believe in the law of the survival of the fittest" as meaning that the stronger shall hold in subjection or "have power to hurt" the simple hearted "weaker." They believe that only Spirit is "fittest." They tell us that Spirit can match Spirit with Joy increasing and Strength perfecting.

So they speak to the responsive Spirit of their patients over and over again the wonderful words of Life announced in Science.

There is no wearying Spirit, there is no depressing or discouraging Spirit.

Buoyancy, Joyousness, Irresistible Energy, are the effects of Spiritual doctrine preached by silent treatment, uttered by sincere lips, or written by loving thinkers.

The spiritual law persistently declared by five consecutive statements to the waiting mind of a patient, will call forth a response from him in harmony with the Truth told, over and above and through and in spite of all that his senses have declared.

He will come with a look of refreshment and health, a look of peace and strength, and the eye of a clean conscience.

Scientific reasoning to so-called sick people, cures them in a three-fold fashion. They must show awakened intelligence, moral purity and bodily health, or they are not yet demonstrably healed. To do less than this for one who comes for treatment is to fall short of the perfect ministry. Sometimes practitioners complain of the formula for dealing with the character quality of people, because they say it stirs them up and irritates them to be treated to be "cleansed from secret faults." But any other treatment is not Christian healing, for Jesus Christ insisted on cleansing from sin as well as disease. "Go and sin no more."

Often a patient under care shows forth one change in a marked degree, while the other changes are slowly coming forward. This is a sign that the practitioner has to deny something in his or her own character.

To be able to promptly put away error we must "cast the beam out of our own eye."

Only the Caleb and Joshua type of mind can choose which condition shall demonstrate first whether health of character, judgment, or body, and see it come forth promptly. The rest have to take it by lot.

Caleb and Joshua never complained of hardships or trials or deprivations, though all the desert marches were as long and hard for them as for the others, but the others "provoked the Lord with their complainings."

If we have provoked the Lord by our complainings we will first redeem our treatments from their colorings of complaint, and then we too can say to the body, Be well; to the judgment, Be perfect; to the character, Be holy.

The simplest hearted house servant can do as perfect healing as the prince of scholars if she speak forth her words from the ground bed of trust in the Absoluteness of The Good.

The ablest preacher will fail if he insists that there is another power battling against The Good, whether he call it the principle of evil or Satan.

Nobody can heal who believes that the principle of evil holds his patient or his fellow beings in bondage. Nobody heals who feels that by his own mortal will, or force, or peculiar fitness, he can do better work than his neighbors.

The Blessed Health Principle knows no respect of persons and allows no divided faith in Her workers.

She takes Her students step-by-step to the gateway of perfect understanding. Then she tells each one to speak for himself the mystic passwords that admit him into understanding.

Some of Her lessons treat of Absolute Spirit. The intellect cannot perceive their import. "The natural man receiveth not the things of the Spirit of God: for they are foolishness unto him: neither can he know them, because they are spiritually discerned."

Spiritual understanding marks absolute power to do the works of God.

"If I do not the works of my Father, believe me not."

The first statements of the Science deny the evidences of the senses, the last statements of Science deny the evidences of the intellect, affirming that only Spiritual perception is true and reliable.

Algazali, the Arabian, in 1058, said:

I began to examine the objects of sensation and speculation to see if they could possibly admit of doubt. Then doubts crowded upon me in such numbers that my incertitude became complete. Whence results the confidence I have in sensible things? The strongest of all our senses is sight, yet if we look at the stars they seem to be as small as money-pieces; but mathematical proofs convince us that they are larger than the earth. These and other things are judged by the senses, but rejected by intellect as false. I abandoned the senses, therefore, having seen my confidence in their absolute truth shaken. Perhaps, said I, there is no assurance but in the notions of intellect reason, that is, first principles, as that ten is more than three?

Upon this the senses replied: 'What assurance have you that your confidence in intellectual reason, is not of the same nature as your confidence in us? When you relied on us, that reason stepped in and gave us the lie; had not intellectual reason been there, you would have continued to rely on us. Well, may there not exist some other judge superior to intellect, who, if he appeared, would refute the judgments of the intellect in the same way that its reasoning refuted us? The non-appearance of such a judge is no proof of his non-existence.'

I strove to answer this objection and my difficulties increased. I said to myself: During sleep you give to vision a reality and existence, and on awakening you are made aware that they were nothing but visions. 'What assurance have you that all you feel and know does actually exist? It seems all true as respects your condition at the moment, but it is nevertheless possible that another condition should represent itself which should be to your awakened state that which your awakened state is now to your sleep, so that, as respects this higher condition, your waking is but sleep.'

Let the best-trained intellects of the round world be gathered to pronounce the death sentence upon the little prince sick with fever. Nothing that their human reason or experience can bring forth gives any hope of life. But the simple-hearted student of Spiritual law comes in and, looking tenderly upon the precious boy, says, "He will live." And the heir of the ages of kingship does live.

There is a power in the Spirit that can cause the mourner to hush. It brings "the oil of joy for mourning and the garment of praise for the spirit of heaviness."

There is a law of Spirit which, by knowing and loving, you can send silent thoughts over the downcast and weary that shall refresh like ocean breezes over heat-burdened travelers. "They shall renew their strength."

There is a word of Absolute Good which, if you learn it, will separate anger and resentment quite away from your mind forever.

Sharper than steel is the sword of the Spirit,

Swifter than arrows the word of the Truth is.

Stronger than anger is love, and subdueth.

"To the dividing asunder of the joints and marrow."

One who has received five divinely true messages from the earnest mind of a Spiritually awakened friend, will find his thought taken quite away from feeling that he dwells in a prison of clay, a house of sorrow.

He will show interest in the help of his follow-men and women. He will acknowledge his own healthy freedom from pain, sleeplessness, discouragement.

It is a signal for warm, fervent, spiritual affirmations when the soul bloom of charity speaks forth from the hitherto closed lips.

As the season advances over the closed bud to its blooming time, the sun shines hotter and hotter.

Speak the words that will feed and satisfy the opening bloom of life and love and health and charity.

Nobody is too healthy or too wise or too good to be blessed by the full strength of the sixth treatment in Christian Science.

While people seem to need to have errors denied, they often refuse to hear the sixth message. It seems like putting the early June bud under the July or August sun.

Find out men's wants and will

And meet them there;

All other joys go less

To the one joy of doing what is best.

Jesus taught the denial of errors (sins). When an object reflects all the colors of the sunshine, we say it is white. When a character is manifestly and acknowledgedly clean, we say it is holy.

Praise in fullest measure the patient who is interested in the welfare of others. Praise that one who acknowledges restored health. Praise that one whom you perceive to be healed, even when he does not admit it. The highest praise you can give is the sixth treatment.

Maybe you must give the sixth treatment to a patient the first time you meet him.

Your own judgment will tell you accurately. Your own judgment is best for yourself. Do not for a moment suppose that somebody else's judgment is necessary to your work.

"If any among you lack wisdom, let him ask of God."

Jesus Christ said to those whom he had faithfully taught concerning their own greatness and glory; "Henceforth I call you not servants, but friends; for all things, that I have heard from the Father I have told you."

A servant is one who obeys another rather than himself.

It makes a vast difference to the calibre and quality of our mental presence what we believe in, whether in our own strength or weakness, our own worth or worthlessness.

As Spirit we are Omnipotence. We must not believe in the inferiority of ourselves to others.

The teachings of the inferiority and superiority of one under or over another have brought about the conflict of caste, and the dissensions of nations. "Hath not one God made you? .... Of one blood all the nations?"

"Love thyself last" is poor policy, as the scorn and cringing of multitudes demonstrate. Unconsciously we have known that there is something wrong about such doctrine. "I glorify myself" is Jesus Christ in you as Redeemer forever from poverty, foolishness, pain, grief, sickness. The Self is God.

I searched for God with heart-throbs of despair

'Neath ocean's bed, above the vaulted sky;

At last I searched myself — my inmost I

And found Him there.

"Love thy neighbor as thy Self."

"I put true words after my I AM, and my world is heaven."

Many a patient has waited the full moving of the waters of Truth concerning his birthright of glory and greatness, as a harmonious chord waits in the silence for a skillful hand to wake it, or as the lame man at the pool longed for the angel to "trouble the waters."

We must recognize all our thoughts as Good. Our thoughts are our work. Our workmanship is always the outpicturing of our thoughts.

When Jesus enjoined the denial of self he did not mean the denial of the good Self, the God Self.

We must recognize the effect of our treatments as perfect. "And God saw everything that he had made; and behold, it was very good."

God is the Eternal Mind. As Mind, acting according to the nature of Mind, all the work of God is pure thinking.

We are the work of God, or the work of Mind. Thus we are the Idea of Mind. As ideas always reflect their thinker in character and office, so we as Idea of God, reflect, or shed abroad the character and office of Our Thinker. THERE IS ONLY ONE GOD. His Character—PERFECTION; HOLINESS. "Be ye Perfect as your Father is Perfect." "Be ye Holy as I AM HOLY."

His office — WORK. "My Father worketh hitherto, and I work." "Establish thou the work of our hands upon us, yea, the work of our hands, establish thou it." "Hands" are efficient thoughts.

Jesus Christ declared that his work was finished when he had shown his companions their equality with himself.

"The glory which Thou gavest me I have given them."

"He that hath seen Me hath seen The Father."

"I and the Father are One."

"I in them and Thou in Me."

"I have finished the work which Thou gavest me to do."

"Ye are the light of the world"

"Call no man upon earth your father, for One is Your Father, even God."

There is no separation of each of us from the other. Each one is our own thought made visible. To praise and honor him or her is to make our thoughts all glorious like as the God Idea that we name them. This final treatment expresses the description of our own thoughts which we should make. To my patient, who acknowledged herself perfectly well, I said, while profoundly recognizing her as my own God Idea made visible:

You are the perfect creation of the living God — spiritual, harmonious, free, fearless.

You reflect all the universe of Good.

From every direction everywhere come the words of Truth, making you to know that you are perfect in Peace, Wisdom, Health, and causing you to show forth Peace, Wisdom, Health, always, world without end.

You reflect All Good from those around you, and show forth to them always, Peace, Wisdom, Health.

From me you reflect Goodness, Peace, Love, Health and Truth, and you shall forever show forth to me Peace, Wisdom, Health.

Life, Truth, Love, Spirit, surround you and sustain you and bear you on in Goodness.

You are peaceful and free and strong and courageous and bold and brave and efficient. You are able to do each day all the work that belongs to you to do — God working in you and through you and by you and for you to bless the world.

You are a living witness of the power of the loving Truth to set free into Health and Strength and living service for the world.

In the name of the Father, and of the Son, and of the Holy Spirit, I pronounce you well and strong and perfect as God made you.

So we must recognize every one unto whom we have given the words of Truth as perfect, without blemish; children indeed of One Common Father. There is no rich or poor, bond or free, high or low in Truth. ALL IS ONE. THERE IS ONLY ONE. WE ARE ONE. *–ech*

## Other Books by Emma Curtis Hopkins

- Bible Interpretations
- Esoteric Philosophy in Spiritual Science
- Genesis Series
- Gospel Series (Sanctuary of Truth)
- High Mysticism
- Judgment Series in Spiritual Science (Sanctuary of Truth)
- Resume
- Scientific Christian Mental Practice  (DeVorss)

## Books About Emma Curtis Hopkins

- Emma Curtis Hopkins, Forgotten Founder of New Thought – Gail Harney
- Unveiling Your Hidden Power: Emma Curtis Hopkins' Metaphysics for the 21st Century – Ruth L. Miller

To find more of Emma's work, including some previously unpublished material, go to:

www.emmacurtishopkins.org

# WISEWOMAN PRESS

1521 N Jantzen Rd. $143
Portland, Oregon  97217
www.wisewomanpress.com

*by Emma Curtis Hopkins*

- The Gospel Series
- Resume

*by Ruth L. Miller*

- A Book of Uncommon Praye
- 150 Years of Healing: The Founders and Science of New Thought
- Unveiling Your Hidden Power: Emma Curtis Hopkins' Metaphysics for the 21st Century

**Watch our website for release dates
and order information!**

www.wisewomanpress.com

7655615R0

Made in the USA
Charleston, SC
27 March 2011